Ready Not

for use with

Fundamentals of Corporate Finance

Sixth Edition

Stephen A. Ross
Massachusetts Institute of Technology

Randolph W. Westerfield
University of Southern California

Bradford D. Jordan
University of Kentucky

Prepared by
Cheri Etling
University of Tampa

Boston   Burr Ridge, IL   Dubuque, IA   Madison, WI   New York   San Francisco   St. Louis
Bangkok   Bogotá   Caracas   Kuala Lumpur   Lisbon   London   Madrid   Mexico City
Milan   Montreal   New Delhi   Santiago   Seoul   Singapore   Sydney   Taipei   Toronto

McGraw-Hill Higher Education

A Division of The McGraw·Hill Companies

Ready Notes for use with
FUNDAMENTALS OF CORPORATE FINANCE
Stephen A. Ross, Randolph W. Westerfield, Bradford D. Jordan

Published by McGraw-Hill/Irwin, an imprint of The McGraw-Hill Companies, Inc., 1221 Avenue of the Americas, New York, NY 10020. Copyright © 2003, 2000, 1998, 1995, 1993, 1991 by The McGraw-Hill Companies, Inc. All rights reserved.
No part of this publication may be reproduced or distributed in any form or by any means, or stored in a database or retrieval system, without the prior written consent of The McGraw-Hill Companies, Inc., including, but not limited to, in any network or other electronic storage or transmission, or broadcast for distance learning.

1 2 3 4 5 6 7 8 9 0 QPD/QPD 0 9 8 7 6 5 4 3 2

ISBN 0-07-246975-7

www.mhhe.com

1.1 Key Concepts and Skills

- Know the basic types of financial management decisions and the role of the financial manager
- Know the financial implications of the different forms of business organization
- Know the goal of financial management
- Understand the conflicts of interest that can arise between owners and managers
- Understand the various types of financial markets

1.2 Chapter Outline

- Corporate Finance and the Financial Manager
- Forms of Business Organization
- The Goal of Financial Management
- The Agency Problem and Control of the Corporation
- Financial Markets and the Corporation

1.3 Corporate Finance

- Some important questions that are answered using finance
  - What long-term investments should the firm take on?
  - Where will we get the long-term financing to pay for the investment?
  - How will we manage the everyday financial activities of the firm?

1.4 Financial Manager

- Financial managers try to answer some or all of these questions
- The top financial manager within a firm is usually the Chief Financial Officer (CFO)
  - Treasurer – oversees cash management, credit management, capital expenditures and financial planning
  - Controller – oversees taxes, cost accounting, financial accounting and data processing

1.5 Financial Management Decisions

- Capital budgeting
  - What long-term investments or projects should the business take on?
- Capital structure
  - How should we pay for our assets?
  - Should we use debt or equity?
- Working capital management
  - How do we manage the day-to-day finances of the firm?

1.6 Forms of Business Organization

- Three major forms in the united states
  - Sole proprietorship
  - Partnership
    - General
    - Limited
  - Corporation
    - S-Corp
    - Limited liability company

1.7 Sole Proprietorship

- Advantages
  - Easiest to start
  - Least regulated
  - Single owner keeps all the profits
  - Taxed once as personal income

- Disadvantages
  - Limited to life of owner
  - Equity capital limited to owner's personal wealth
  - Unlimited liability
  - Difficult to sell ownership interest

1.8 Partnership

- Advantages
  - Two or more owners
  - More capital available
  - Relatively easy to start
  - Income taxed once as personal income

- Disadvantages
  - Unlimited liability
    - General partnership
    - Limited partnership
  - Partnership dissolves when one partner dies or wishes to sell
  - Difficult to transfer ownership

1.9 Corporation

- Advantages
  - Limited liability
  - Unlimited life
  - Separation of ownership and management
  - Transfer of ownership is easy
  - Easier to raise capital

- Disadvantages
  - Separation of ownership and management
  - Double taxation (income taxed at the corporate rate and then dividends taxed at personal rate)

1.10 Goal Of Financial Management

- What should be the goal of a corporation?
  - Maximize profit?
  - Minimize costs?
  - Maximize market share?
  - Maximize the current value of the company's stock?
- Does this mean we should do anything and everything to maximize owner wealth?

1.11 The Agency Problem

- Agency relationship
  - Principal hires an agent to represent their interest
  - Stockholders (principals) hire managers (agents) to run the company
- Agency problem
  - Conflict of interest between principal and agent
- Management goals and agency costs

1.12 Managing Managers

- Managerial compensation
  - Incentives can be used to align management and stockholder interests
  - The incentives need to be structured carefully to make sure that they achieve their goal
- Corporate control
  - The threat of a takeover may result in better management
- Other stakeholders

1.13 Work the Web Example

- The Internet provides a wealth of information about individual companies
- One excellent site is finance.yahoo.com
- Click on the web surfer to go to the site, choose a company and see what information you can find!

1.14 Financial Markets

- Cash flows to the firm
- Primary vs. secondary markets
  - Dealer vs. auction markets
  - Listed vs. over the counter securities
    - NYSE
    - NASDAQ

1.15 Quick Quiz

- What are the three types of financial management decisions and what questions are they designed to answer?
- What are the three major forms of business organization?
- What is the goal of financial management?
- What are agency problems and why do they exist within a corporation?
- What is the difference between a primary market and a secondary market?

2.1 Key Concepts and Skills

- Know the difference between book value and market value
- Know the difference between accounting income and cash flow
- Know the difference between average and marginal tax rates
- Know how to determine a firm's cash flow from its financial statements

2.2 Chapter Outline

- The Balance Sheet
- The Income Statement
- Taxes
- Cash Flow

2.3 Balance Sheet

- The balance sheet is a snapshot of the firm's assets and liabilities at a given point in time
- Assets are listed in order of liquidity
  - Ease of conversion to cash
  - Without significant loss of value
- Balance Sheet Identity
  - Assets = Liabilities + Stockholders' Equity

2.4 The Balance Sheet - Figure 2.1

Total Value of Assets
- Current assets
- Fixed assets
  1. Tangible fixed assets
  2. Intangible fixed assets

Total Value of Liabilities and Shareholders' Equity
- Current liabilities
- Long-term debt
- Shareholders' equity

Net working capital

2.5 Net Working Capital and Liquidity

- Net Working Capital
  - Current Assets − Current Liabilities
  - Positive when the cash that will be received over the next 12 months exceeds the cash that will be paid out
  - Usually positive in a healthy firm
- Liquidity
  - Ability to convert to cash quickly without a significant loss in value
  - Liquid firms are less likely to experience financial distress
  - But, liquid assets earn a lower return
  - Trade to find balance between liquid and illiquid assets

2.6 US Corporation Balance Sheet – Table 2.1

U.S. CORPORATION
Balance Sheets as of December 31, 2001 and 2002
($ in millions)

Assets	2001	2002	Liabilities and Owners' Equity	2001	2002
Current assets			**Current liabilities**		
Cash	$ 104	$ 160	Accounts payable	$ 232	$ 266
Accounts receivable	455	688	Notes payable	196	123
Inventory	553	555	Total	$ 428	$ 389
Total	$1,112	$1,403			
Fixed assets					
Net plant and equipment	$1,644	$1,709	Long-term debt	$ 408	$ 454
			Owners' equity		
			Common stock and paid-in surplus	600	640
			Retained earnings	1,320	1,629
			Total	$1,920	$2,269
Total assets	$2,756	$3,112	Total liabilities and owners' equity	$2,756	$3,112

2.7 Market Vs. Book Value

- The balance sheet provides the book value of the assets, liabilities and equity.
- Market value is the price at which the assets, liabilities or equity can actually be bought or sold.
- Market value and book value are often very different. Why?
- Which is more important to the decision-making process?

2.8 Example 2.2 Klingon Corporation

KLINGON CORPORATION					
Balance Sheets					
Market Value versus Book Value					
	Book	Market		Book	Market
Assets			Liabilities and Shareholders' Equity		
NWC	$ 400	$ 600	LTD	$ 500	$ 500
NFA	700	1,000	SE	600	1,100
	1,100	1,600		1,100	1,600

Income Statement

- The income statement is more like a video of the firm's operations for a specified period of time.
- You generally report revenues first and then deduct any expenses for the period
- Matching principle – GAAP say to show revenue when it accrues and match the expenses required to generate the revenue

US Corporation Income Statement – Table 2.2

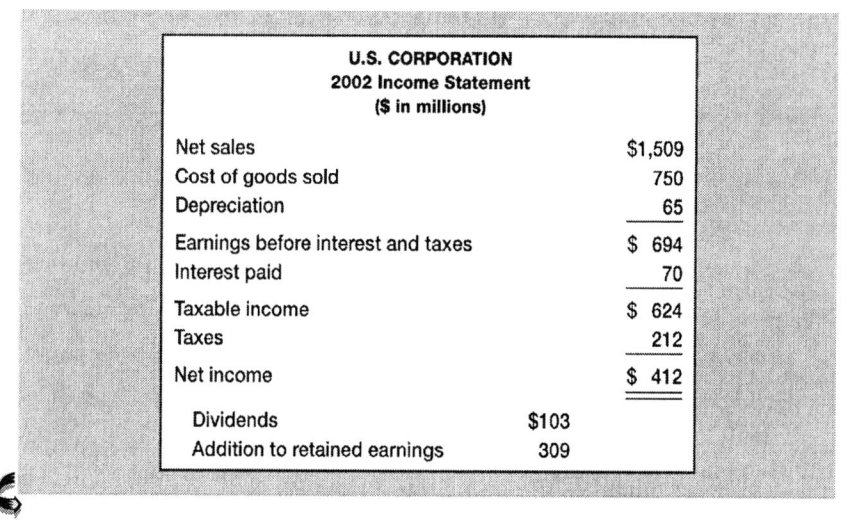

U.S. CORPORATION
2002 Income Statement
($ in millions)

Net sales	$1,509
Cost of goods sold	750
Depreciation	65
Earnings before interest and taxes	$ 694
Interest paid	70
Taxable income	$ 624
Taxes	212
Net income	$ 412
Dividends	$103
Addition to retained earnings	309

2.11 Work the Web Example

- Publicly traded companies must file regular reports with the Securities and Exchange Commission
- These reports are usually filed electronically and can be searched at the SEC public site called EDGAR
- Click on the web surfer, pick a company and see what you can find!

2.12 Taxes

- The one thing we can rely on with taxes is that they are always changing
- Marginal vs. average tax rates
  - Marginal – the percentage paid on the next dollar earned
  - Average – the tax bill / taxable income
- Other taxes

2.13 Example: Marginal Vs. Average Rates

- Suppose your firm earns $4 million in taxable income.
    - What is the firm's tax liability?
    - What is the average tax rate?
    - What is the marginal tax rate?
- If you are considering a project that will increase the firm's taxable income by $1 million, what tax rate should you use in your analysis?

2.14 The Concept of Cash Flow

- Cash flow is one of the most important pieces of information that a financial manager can derive from financial statements
- The statement of cash flows does not provide us with the same information that we are looking at here
- We will look at how cash is generated from utilizing assets and how it is paid to those that finance the purchase of the assets

2.15 Cash Flow From Assets

- Cash Flow From Assets (CFFA) = Cash Flow to Creditors + Cash Flow to Stockholders
- Cash Flow From Assets = Operating Cash Flow – Net Capital Spending – Changes in NWC

2.16 Example: US Corporation

- OCF (I/S) = EBIT + depreciation – taxes = $547
- NCS (B/S and I/S) = ending net fixed assets – beginning net fixed assets + depreciation = $130
- Changes in NWC (B/S) = ending NWC – beginning NWC = $330
- CFFA = 547 – 130 – 330 = $87
- CF to Creditors (B/S and I/S) = interest paid – net new borrowing = $24
- CF to Stockholders (B/S and I/S) = dividends paid – net new equity raised = $63
- CFFA = 24 + 63 = $87

2.17 Cash Flow Summary Table 2.5

I. **The cash flow identity**
   Cash flow from assets = Cash flow to creditors (bondholders)
                                        + Cash flow to stockholders (owners)

II. **Cash flow from assets**
   Cash flow from assets = Operating cash flow
                                − Net capital spending
                                − Change in net working capital (NWC)
   where:
   Operating cash flow = Earnings before interest and taxes (EBIT)
                                     + Depreciation − Taxes
   Net capital spending = Ending net fixed assets − Beginning net fixed assets
                                      + Depreciation
   Change in NWC = Ending NWC − Beginning NWC

III. **Cash flow to creditors (bondholders)**
   Cash flow to creditors = Interest paid − Net new borrowing

IV. **Cash flow to stockholders (owners)**
   Cash flow to stockholders = Dividends paid − Net new equity raised

2.18 Example: Balance Sheet and Income Statement Information

- Current Accounts
  - 1998: CA = 4500; CL = 1300
  - 1999: CA = 2000; CL = 1700
- Fixed Assets and Depreciation
  - 1998: NFA = 3000; 1999: NFA = 4000
  - Depreciation expense = 300
- LT Liabilities and Equity
  - 1998: LTD = 2200; Common Equity = 500; RE = 500
  - 1999: LTD = 2800; Common Equity = 750; RE = 750
- Income Statement Information
  - EBIT = 2700; Interest Expense = 200; Taxes = 1000; Dividends = 1250

Example: Cash Flows

- OCF = 2700 + 300 − 1000 = 2000
- NCS = 4000 − 3000 + 300 = 1300
- Changes in NWC = (2000 − 1700) − (1500 − 1300) = 100
- CFFA = 2000 − 1300 − 100 = 600
- CF to Creditors = 200 − (2800 − 2200) = -400
- CF to Stockholders = 1250 − (750 − 500) = 1000
- CFFA = -400 + 1000 = 600
- The CF identity holds.

Quick Quiz

- What is the difference between book value and market value? Which should we use for decision making purposes?
- What is the difference between accounting income and cash flow? Which do we need to use when making decisions?
- What is the difference between average and marginal tax rates? Which should we use when making financial decisions?
- How do we determine a firm's cash flows? What are the equations and where do we find the information?

3.1 Key Concepts and Skills

- Understand sources and uses of cash and the Statement of Cash Flows
- Know how to standardize financial statements for comparison purposes
- Know how to compute and interpret important financial ratios
- Be able to compute and interpret the Du Pont Identity
- Understand the problems and pitfalls in financial statement analysis

3.2 Chapter Outline

- Cash Flow and Financial Statements: A Closer Look
- Standardized Financial Statements
- Ratio Analysis
- The Du Pont Identity
- Using Financial Statement Information

3.3 Sample Balance Sheet

Numbers in thousands

	2000	1999		2000	1999
Cash & Equivalents	3,171	6,489	A/P	313,286	340,220
A/R	1,095,118	1,048,991	N/P	227,848	86,631
Inventory	388,947	295,255	Other CL	1,239,651	1,098,602
Other CA	314,454	232,304	Total CL	1,780,785	1,525,453
Total CA	1,801,690	1,583,039	LT Debt	1,389,615	871,851
Net FA	3,129,754	2,535,072	C/S	1,761,044	1,648,490
Total Assets	4,931,444	4,118,111	Total Liab. & Equity	4,931,444	4,118,111

3.4 Sample Income Statement

Numbers in thousands, except EPS & DPS

Revenues	4,335,491
Cost of Goods Sold	1,762,721
Expenses	1,390,262
Depreciation	362,325
EBIT	820,183
Interest Expense	52,841
Taxable Income	767,342
Taxes	295,426
Net Income	471,916
EPS	2.41
Dividends per share	0.93

3.5 Sources and Uses

- Sources
  - Cash inflow – occurs when we "sell" something
  - Decrease in asset account (Sample B/S)
    - Cash & equivalents is the only source
  - Increase in liability or equity account
    - Everything except accounts payable is a source
- Uses
  - Cash outflow – occurs when we "buy" something
  - Increase in asset account
    - Everything except cash & equivalents is a use
  - Decrease in liability or equity account
    - Accounts payable is the only use

3.6 Statement of Cash Flows

- Statement that summarizes the sources and uses of cash
- Changes divided into three major categories
  - Operating Activity – includes net income and changes in most current accounts
  - Investment Activity – includes changes in fixed assets
  - Financing Activity – includes changes in notes payable, long-term debt and equity accounts as well as dividends

3.7 Sample Statement of Cash Flows

Numbers in thousands

Cash, beginning of year	6,489	Financing Activity	
Operating Activity		Increase in Notes Payable	141,217
Net Income	471,916	Increase in LT Debt	517,764
Plus: Depreciation	362,325	Decrease in C/S	-36,159
Increase in Other CL	141,049	Dividends Paid	-395,521
Less: Increase in A/R	-46,127	Net Cash from Financing	227,301
Increase in Inventory	-93,692	Net Decrease in Cash	-3,319
Increase in Other CA	-82,150	Cash End of Year	3,170*
Decrease in A/P	-26,934		
Net Cash from Operations	726,387		
Investment Activity			
Fixed Asset Acquisition	-957,007		
Net Cash from Investments	-957,007	*Difference due to rounding of dividends	

3.8 Standardized Financial Statements

- Common-Size Balance Sheets
  - Compute all accounts as a percent of total assets
- Common-Size Income Statements
  - Compute all line items as a percent of sales
- Standardized statements make it easier to compare financial information, particularly as the company grows
- They are also useful for comparing companies of different sizes, particularly within the same industry

3.9 Ratio Analysis

- Ratios also allow for better comparison through time or between companies
- As we look at each ratio, ask yourself what the ratio is trying to measure and why is that information important
- Ratios are used both internally and externally

3.10 Categories of Financial Ratios

- Short-term solvency or liquidity ratios
- Long-term solvency or financial leverage ratios
- Asset management or turnover ratios
- Profitability ratios
- Market value ratios

3.11 Computing Liquidity Ratios

- Current Ratio = CA / CL
  - 1,801,690 / 1,780,785 = 1.01 times
- Quick Ratio = (CA − Inventory) / CL
  - (1,801,690 − 314,454) / 1,780,785 = .835 times
- Cash Ratio = Cash / CL
  - 3,171 / 1,780,785 = .002 times

3.12 Computing Long-term Solvency Ratios

- Total Debt Ratio = (TA − TE) / TA
  - (4,931,444 − 1,761,044) / 4,931,444 = .6429 times or 64.29%
  - The firm finances a little over 64% of its assets with debt.
- Debt/Equity = TD / TE
  - (4,931,444 − 1,761,044) / 1,761,044 = 1.800 times
- Equity Multiplier = TA / TE = 1 + D/E
  - 1 + 1.800 = 2.800

3.13 Computing Coverage Ratios

- Times Interest Earned = EBIT / Interest
  - 820,183 / 52,841 = 15.5 times
- Cash Coverage = (EBIT + Depreciation) / Interest
  - (820,183 + 362,325) / 52,841 = 22.38 times

3.14 Computing Inventory Ratios

- Inventory Turnover = Cost of Goods Sold / Inventory
  - 1,762,721 / 388,947 = 4.53 times
- Days' Sales in Inventory = 365 / Inventory Turnover
  - 365 / 4.53 = 81 days

3.15 Computing Receivables Ratios

- Receivables Turnover = Sales / Accounts Receivable
  - 4,335,491 / 1,095,118 = 3.96 times
- Days' Sales in Receivables = 365 / Receivables Turnover
  - 365 / 3.96 = 92 days

3.16 Computing Total Asset Turnover

- Total Asset Turnover = Sales / Total Assets
  - 4,335,491 / 4,931,444 = .88 times
- Measure of asset use efficiency
- Not unusual for TAT < 1, especially if a firm has a large amount of fixed assets

Computing Profitability Measures

- Profit Margin = Net Income / Sales
  - 471,916 / 4,335,491 = .1088 times or 10.88%
- Return on Assets (ROA) = Net Income / Total Assets
  - 471,916 / 4,931,444 = .0957 times or 9.57%
- Return on Equity (ROE) = Net Income / Total Equity
  - 471,916 / 1,761,044 = .2680 times or 26.8%

Computing Market Value Measures

- Market Price = $60.98 per share
- Shares outstanding = 205,838,910
- PE Ratio = Price per share / Earnings per share
  - 60.98 / 2.41 = 25.3 times
- Market-to-book ratio = market value per share / book value per share
  - 60.98 / (1,761,044,000 / 205,838,910) = 7.1 times

3.19 Deriving the Du Pont Identity

- ROE = NI / TE
- Multiply by 1 and then rearrange
  - ROE = (NI / TE) (TA / TA)
  - ROE = (NI / TA) (TA / TE) = ROA * EM
- Multiply by 1 again and then rearrange
  - ROE = (NI / TA) (TA / TE) (Sales / Sales)
  - ROE = (NI / Sales) (Sales / TA) (TA / TE)
  - ROE = PM * TAT * EM

3.20 Using the Du Pont Identity

- ROE = PM * TAT * EM
  - Profit margin is a measure of the firm's operating efficiency – how well does it control costs
  - Total asset turnover is a measure of the firm's asset use efficiency – how well does it manage its assets
  - Equity multiplier is a measure of the firm's financial leverage

3.21 Why Evaluate Financial Statements?

- Internal uses
  - Performance evaluation – compensation and comparison between divisions
  - Planning for the future – guide in estimating future cash flows
- External uses
  - Creditors
  - Suppliers
  - Customers
  - Stockholders

3.22 Benchmarking

- Ratios are not very helpful by themselves; they need to be compared to something
- Time-Trend Analysis
  - Used to see how the firm's performance is changing through time
  - Internal and external uses
- Peer Group Analysis
  - Compare to similar companies or within industries
  - SIC and NAICS codes

3.23 Real World Example - I

- Ratios are figured using financial data from the 1999 Annual Report for Ethan Allen
- Compare the ratios to the industry ratios in Table 3.9 in the book
- Ethan Allen's fiscal year end is June 30.
- Be sure to note how the ratios are computed in the table so that you can compute comparable numbers.
- Ethan Allan sales = $762 MM

3.24 Real World Example - II

- Liquidity ratios
  - Current ratio = 2.433x; Industry = 1.4x
  - Quick ratio = .763x; Industry = .6x
- Long-term solvency ratio
  - Debt/Equity ratio (Debt / Worth) = .371x; Industry = 1.9x.
- Coverage ratio
  - Times Interest Earned = 70.6x; Industry = 3.4x

Real World Example - III

- Asset management ratios:
  - Inventory turnover = 2.8x; Industry = 3.6x
  - Receivables turnover = 22.2x (16 days); Industry = 17.7x (21 days)
  - Total asset turnover = 1.6x; Industry = 2.2x
- Profitability ratios
  - Profit margin before taxes = 17.4%; Industry = 3.1%
  - ROA (profit before taxes / total assets) = 27.6%; Industry = 5.8%
  - ROE = (profit before taxes / tangible net worth) = 37.9%; Industry = 17.6%

Potential Problems

- There is no underlying theory, so there is no way to know which ratios are most relevant
- Benchmarking is difficult for diversified firms
- Globalization and international competition makes comparison more difficult because of differences in accounting regulations
- Varying accounting procedures, i.e. FIFO vs. LIFO
- Different fiscal years
- Extraordinary events

3.27 Work the Web Example

- The Internet makes ratio analysis much easier than it has been in the past
- Click on the web surfer to go to Multex Investor
  - Choose a company and enter its ticker symbol
  - Click on comparison and see what information is available

3.28 Quick Quiz

- What is the Statement of Cash Flows and how do you determine sources and uses of cash?
- How do you standardize balance sheets and income statements and why is standardization useful?
- What are the major categories of ratios and how do you compute specific ratios within each category?
- What are some of the problems associated with financial statement analysis?

4.1 Key Concepts and Skills

- Understand the financial planning process and how decisions are interrelated
- Be able to develop a financial plan using the percentage of sales approach
- Understand the four major decision areas involved in long-term financial planning
- Understand how capital structure policy and dividend policy affect a firm's ability to grow

4.2 Chapter Outline

- What is Financial Planning?
- Financial Planning Models: A First Look
- The Percentage of Sales Approach
- External Financing and Growth
- Some Caveats Regarding Financial Planning Models

4.3 Elements of Financial Planning

- Investment in new assets – determined by capital budgeting decisions
- Degree of financial leverage – determined by capital structure decisions
- Cash paid to shareholders – dividend policy decisions
- Liquidity requirements – determined by net working capital decisions

4.4 Financial Planning Process

- Planning Horizon - divide decisions into short-run decisions (usually next 12 months) and long-run decisions (usually 2 – 5 years)
- Aggregation - combine capital budgeting decisions into one big project
- Assumptions and Scenarios
  - Make realistic assumptions about important variables
  - Run several scenarios where you vary the assumptions by reasonable amounts
  - Determine at least a worst case, normal case and best case scenario

4.5 Role of Financial Planning

- Examining interactions – helps management see the interactions between decisions
- Exploring options – gives management a systematic framework for exploring its opportunities
- Avoiding surprises – helps management identify possible outcomes and plan accordingly
- Ensuring Feasibility and Internal Consistency – helps management determine if goals can be accomplished and if the various stated (and unstated) goals of the firm are consistent with one another

4.6 Financial Planning Model Ingredients

- Sales Forecast – many cash flows depend directly on the level of sales (often estimated using a growth rate in sales)
- Pro Forma Statements – setting up the plan as projected financial statements allows for consistency and ease of interpretation
- Asset Requirements – how much additional fixed assets will be required to meet sales projections
- Financial Requirements – how much financing will we need to pay for the required assets
- Plug Variable – management decision about what type of financing will be used (makes the balance sheet balance)
- Economic Assumptions – explicit assumptions about the coming economic environment

4.7 Example: Historical Financial Statements

Gourmet Coffee Inc.
Balance Sheet
December 31, 2001

Assets	1000	Debt	400
		Equity	600
Total	1000	Total	1000

Gourmet Coffee Inc.
Income Statement
For Year Ended
December 31, 2001

Revenues	2000
Costs	1600
Net Income	400

4.8 Example: Pro Forma Income Statement

- Initial Assumptions
  - Revenues will grow at 15% (2000*1.15)
  - All items are tied directly to sales and the current relationships are optimal
  - Consequently, all other items will also grow at 15%

Gourmet Coffee Inc.
Pro Forma Income Statement
For Year Ended 2002

Revenues	2,300
Costs	1,840
Net Income	460

4.9 Example: Pro Forma Balance Sheet

- Case I
  - Dividends are the plug variable, so equity increases at 15%
  - Dividends = 460 NI – 90 increase in equity = 370
- Case II
  - Debt is the plug variable and no dividends are paid
  - Debt = 1,150 – (600+460) = 90
  - Repay 400 – 90 = 310 in debt

Gourmet Coffee Inc.
Pro Forma Balance Sheet
Case 1

Assets	1,150	Debt	460
		Equity	690
Total	1,150	Total	1,150

Gourmet Coffee Inc.
Pro Forma Balance Sheet
Case 1

Assets	1,150	Debt	90
		Equity	1,060
Total	1,150	Total	1,150

4.10 Percent of Sales Approach

- Some items tend to vary directly with sales, while others do not
- Income Statement
  - Costs may vary directly with sales
  - If this is the case, then the profit margin is constant
  - Dividends are a management decision and generally do not vary directly with sales – this affects the retained earnings that go on the balance sheet
- Balance Sheet
  - Initially assume that all assets, including fixed, vary directly with sales
  - Accounts payable will also normally vary directly with sales
  - Notes payable, long-term debt and equity generally do not because they depend on management decisions about capital structure
  - The change in the retained earnings portion of equity will come from the dividend decision

4.11 Example: Income Statement

Tasha's Toy Emporium
Income Statement, 2001

		% of Sales
Sales	5,000	
Costs	3,000	60%
EBT	2,000	40%
Taxes (40%)	800	16%
Net Income	1,200	24%
Dividends	600	
Add. To RE	600	

Dividend Payout Rate = 50%

Tasha's Toy Emporium
Pro Forma Income Statement, 2002

Sales	5,500
Costs	3,300
EBT	2,200
Taxes	880
Net Income	1,320
Dividends	660
Add. To RE	660

Assume Sales grow at 10%

4.12 Example: Balance Sheet

Tasha's Toy Emporium – Balance Sheet

	Current	% of Sales	Pro Forma		Current	% of Sales	Pro Forma
ASSETS				**Liabilities & Owners' Equity**			
Current Assets				Current Liabilities			
Cash	$500	10%	$550	A/P	$900	18%	$990
A/R	2,000	40	2,200	N/P	2,500	n/a	2,500
Inventory	3,000	60	3,300	Total	3,400	n/a	3,490
Total	5,500	110	6,050	LT Debt	2,000	n/a	2,000
Fixed Assets				Owners' Equity			
Net PP&E	4,000	80	4,400	CS & APIC	2,000	n/a	2,000
Total Assets	9,500	190	10,450	RE	2,100	n/a	2,760
				Total	4,100	n/a	4,760
				Total L & OE	9,500		10,250

4.13 Example: External Financing Needed

- The firm needs to come up with an additional $200 in debt or equity to make the balance sheet balance
  - TA – TL&OE = 10,450 – 10,250 = 200
- Choose plug variable
  - Borrow more short-term (Notes Payable)
  - Borrow more long-term (LT Debt)
  - Sell more common stock (CS & APIC)
  - Decrease dividend payout, which increase Add. To RE

4.14 Example: Operating at Less than Full Capacity

- Suppose that the company is currently operating at 80% capacity.
  - Full Capacity sales = 5000 / .8 = 6,250
  - Estimated sales = $5,500, so would still only be operating at 88%
  - Therefore, no additional fixed assets would be required.
  - Pro forma Total Assets = 6,050 + 4,000 = 10,050
  - Total Liabilities and Owners' Equity = 10,250
- Choose plug variable
  - Repay some short-term debt (decrease Notes Payable)
  - Repay some long-term debt (decrease LT Debt)
  - Buy back stock (decrease CS & APIC)
  - Pay more in dividends (reduce Add. To RE)
  - Increase cash account

4.15 Work the Web Example

- Looking for estimates of company growth rates?
- What do the analysts have to say?
- Check out Yahoo Finance – click the web surfer, enter a company ticker and follow the "Research" link

4.16 Growth and External Financing

- At low growth levels, internal financing (retained earnings) may exceed the required investment in assets
- As the growth rate increases, the internal financing will not be enough and the firm will have to go to the capital markets for money
- Examining the relationship between growth and external financing required is a useful tool in long-range planning

4.17 The Internal Growth Rate

- The internal growth rate tells us how much the firm can grow assets using retained earnings as the only source of financing.

$$\text{Internal Growth Rate} = \frac{\text{ROA} \times b}{1 - \text{ROA} \times b}$$
$$= \frac{.1041 \times .6037}{1 - .1041 \times .6037} = .0671$$
$$= 6.71\%$$

4.18 The Sustainable Growth Rate

- The sustainable growth rate tells us how much the firm can grow by using internally generated funds and issuing debt to maintain a constant debt ratio.

$$\text{Sustainable Growth Rate} = \frac{\text{ROE} \times b}{1 - \text{ROE} \times b}$$
$$= \frac{.2517 \times .6037}{1 - .2517 \times .6037} = .1792$$
$$= 17.92\%$$

Determinants of Growth

- Profit margin – operating efficiency
- Total asset turnover – asset use efficiency
- Financial leverage – choice of optimal debt ratio
- Dividend policy – choice of how much to pay to shareholders versus reinvesting in the firm

Important Questions

- It is important to remember that we are working with accounting numbers and ask ourselves some important questions as we go through the planning process
- How does our plan affect the timing and risk of our cash flows?
- Does the plan point out inconsistencies in our goals?
- If we follow this plan, will we maximize owners' wealth?

Quick Quiz

- What is the purpose of long-range planning?
- What are the major decision areas involved in developing a plan?
- What is the percentage of sales approach?
- How do you adjust the model when operating at less than full capacity?
- What is the internal growth rate?
- What is the sustainable growth rate?
- What are the major determinants of growth?

5.1 Key Concepts and Skills

- Be able to compute the future value of an investment made today
- Be able to compute the present value of cash to be received at some future date
- Be able to compute the return on an investment
- Be able to compute the number of periods that equates a present value and a future value given an interest rate
- Be able to use a financial calculator and/or a spreadsheet to solve time value of money problems

5.2 Chapter Outline

- Future Value and Compounding
- Present Value and Discounting
- More on Present and Future Values

5.3 Basic Definitions

- Present Value – earlier money on a time line
- Future Value – later money on a time line
- Interest rate – "exchange rate" between earlier money and later money
  - Discount rate
  - Cost of capital
  - Opportunity cost of capital
  - Required return

5.4 Future Values

- Suppose you invest $1000 for one year at 5% per year. What is the future value in one year?
  - Interest = 1000(.05) = 50
  - Value in one year = principal + interest = 1000 + 50 = 1050
  - Future Value (FV) = 1000(1 + .05) = 1050
- Suppose you leave the money in for another year. How much will you have two years from now?
  - FV = $1000(1.05)(1.05) = 1000(1.05)^2 = 1102.50$

5.5 Future Values: General Formula

- $FV = PV(1 + r)^t$
  - FV = future value
  - PV = present value
  - r = period interest rate, expressed as a decimal
  - T = number of periods
- Future value interest factor = $(1 + r)^t$

5.6 Effects of Compounding

- Simple interest
- Compound interest
- Consider the previous example
  - FV with simple interest = 1000 + 50 + 50 = 1100
  - FV with compound interest = 1102.50
  - The extra 2.50 comes from the interest of .05(50) = 2.50 earned on the first interest payment

5.7 Calculator Keys

- Texas Instruments BA-II Plus
  - FV = future value
  - PV = present value
  - I/Y = period interest rate
    - P/Y must equal 1 for the I/Y to be the period rate
    - Interest is entered as a percent, not a decimal
  - N = number of periods
  - Remember to clear the registers (CLR TVM) after each problem
  - Other calculators are similar in format

5.8 Future Values – Example 2

- Suppose you invest the $1000 from the previous example for 5 years. How much would you have?
  - $FV = 1000(1.05)^5 = 1276.28$
- The effect of compounding is small for a small number of periods, but increases as the number of periods increases. (Simple interest would have a future value of $1250, for a difference of $26.28.)

5.9 Future Values – Example 3

- Suppose you had a relative deposit $10 at 5.5% interest 200 years ago. How much would the investment be worth today?
  - FV = $10(1.055)^{200}$ = 447,189.84
- What is the effect of compounding?
  - Simple interest = 10 + 200(10)(.055) = 210.55
  - Compounding added $446,979.29 to the value of the investment

5.10 Future Value as a General Growth Formula

- Suppose your company expects to increase unit sales of widgets by 15% per year for the next 5 years. If you currently sell 3 million widgets in one year, how many widgets do you expect to sell in 5 years?
  - FV = $3,000,000(1.15)^5$ = 6,034,072

5.11 Quick Quiz – Part I

- What is the difference between simple interest and compound interest?
- Suppose you have $500 to invest and you believe that you can earn 8% per year over the next 15 years.
  - How much would you have at the end of 15 years using compound interest?
  - How much would you have using simple interest?

5.12 Present Values

- How much do I have to invest today to have some amount in the future?
  - $FV = PV(1 + r)^t$
  - Rearrange to solve for $PV = FV / (1 + r)^t$
- When we talk about discounting, we mean finding the present value of some future amount.
- When we talk about the "value" of something, we are talking about the present value unless we specifically indicate that we want the future value.

5.13 Present Value – One Period Example

- Suppose you need $10,000 in one year for the down payment on a new car. If you can earn 7% annually, how much do you need to invest today?
- PV = $10,000 / (1.07)^1 = 9345.79$
- Calculator
  - 1 N
  - 7 I/Y
  - 10,000 FV
  - CPT PV = -9345.79

5.14 Present Values – Example 2

- You want to begin saving for you daughter's college education and you estimate that she will need $150,000 in 17 years. If you feel confident that you can earn 8% per year, how much do you need to invest today?
  - PV = $150,000 / (1.08)^{17} = 40,540.34$

5.15 Present Values – Example 3

- Your parents set up a trust fund for you 10 years ago that is now worth $19,671.51. If the fund earned 7% per year, how much did your parents invest?
  - PV = $19,671.51 / (1.07)^{10}$ = 10,000

5.16 Present Value – Important Relationship I

- For a given interest rate – the longer the time period, the lower the present value
  - What is the present value of $500 to be received in 5 years? 10 years? The discount rate is 10%
  - 5 years: PV = $500 / (1.1)^5$ = 310.46
  - 10 years: PV = $500 / (1.1)^{10}$ = 192.77

5.17 Present Value – Important Relationship II

- For a given time period – the higher the interest rate, the smaller the present value
  - What is the present value of $500 received in 5 years if the interest rate is 10%? 15%?
    - Rate = 10%: PV = $500 / (1.1)^5 = 310.46$
    - Rate = 15%; PV = $500 / (1.15)^5 = 248.58$

5.18 Quick Quiz – Part II

- What is the relationship between present value and future value?
- Suppose you need $15,000 in 3 years. If you can earn 6% annually, how much do you need to invest today?
- If you could invest the money at 8%, would you have to invest more or less than at 6%? How much?

The Basic PV Equation - Refresher

- $PV = FV / (1 + r)^t$
- There are four parts to this equation
  - PV, FV, r and t
  - If we know any three, we can solve for the fourth
- If you are using a financial calculator, be sure and remember the sign convention or you will receive an error when solving for r or t

Discount Rate

- Often we will want to know what the implied interest rate is in an investment
- Rearrange the basic PV equation and solve for r
  - $FV = PV(1 + r)^t$
  - $r = (FV / PV)^{1/t} - 1$
- If you are using formulas, you will want to make use of both the y^x and the $1/x$ keys

Discount Rate – Example 1

- You are looking at an investment that will pay $1200 in 5 years if you invest $1000 today. What is the implied rate of interest?
    - $r = (1200 / 1000)^{1/5} - 1 = .03714 = 3.714\%$
    - Calculator – the sign convention matters!!!
        - N = 5
        - PV = -1000 (you pay 1000 today)
        - FV = 1200 (you receive 1200 in 5 years)
        - CPT I/Y = 3.714%

Discount Rate – Example 2

- Suppose you are offered an investment that will allow you to double your money in 6 years. You have $10,000 to invest. What is the implied rate of interest?
    - $r = (20{,}000 / 10{,}000)^{1/6} - 1 = .122462 = 12.25\%$

5.23 Discount Rate – Example 3

- Suppose you have a 1-year old son and you want to provide $75,000 in 17 years towards his college education. You currently have $5000 to invest. What interest rate must you earn to have the $75,000 when you need it?
  - $r = (75{,}000 / 5{,}000)^{1/17} - 1 = .172688 = 17.27\%$

5.24 Quick Quiz – Part III

- What are some situations where you might want to compute the implied interest rate?
- Suppose you are offered the following investment choices:
  - You can invest $500 today and receive $600 in 5 years. The investment is considered low risk.
  - You can invest the $500 in a bank account paying 4%.
  - What is the implied interest rate for the first choice and which investment should you choose?

Finding the Number of Periods

- Start with basic equation and solve for t (remember your logs)
  - $FV = PV(1 + r)^t$
  - $t = \ln(FV / PV) / \ln(1 + r)$
- You can use the financial keys on the calculator as well, just remember the sign convention.

Number of Periods – Example 1

- You want to purchase a new car and you are willing to pay $20,000. If you can invest at 10% per year and you currently have $15,000, how long will it be before you have enough money to pay cash for the car?
  - $t = \ln(20{,}000 / 15{,}000) / \ln(1.1) = 3.02$ years

5.27 Number of Periods – Example 2

- Suppose you want to buy a new house. You currently have $15,000 and you figure you need to have a 10% down payment plus an additional 5% in closing costs. If the type of house you want costs about $150,000 and you can earn 7.5% per year, how long will it be before you have enough money for the down payment and closing costs?

5.28 Number of Periods – Example 2 Continued

- How much do you need to have in the future?
  - Down payment = .1(150,000) = 15,000
  - Closing costs = .05(150,000 – 15,000) = 6,750
  - Total needed = 15,000 + 6,750 = 21,750
- Compute the number of periods
  - PV = -15,000
  - FV = 21,750
  - I/Y = 7.5
  - CPT N = 5.14 years
- Using the formula
  - t = ln(21,750 / 15,000) / ln(1.075) = 5.14 years

Quick Quiz – Part IV

- When might you want to compute the number of periods?
- Suppose you want to buy some new furniture for your family room. You currently have $500 and the furniture you want costs $600. If you can earn 6%, how long will you have to wait if you don't add any additional money?

Spreadsheet Example

- Use the following formulas for TVM calculations
  - FV(rate,nper,pmt,pv)
  - PV(rate,nper,pmt,fv)
  - RATE(nper,pmt,pv,fv)
  - NPER(rate,pmt,pv,fv)

- The formula icon is very useful when you can't remember the exact formula
- Click on the Excel icon to open a spreadsheet containing four different examples.

Work the Web Example

- Many financial calculators are available online
- Click on the web surfer to go to Cigna's web site and work the following example:
  - You need $50,000 in 10 years. If you can earn 6% interest, how much do you need to invest today?
  - You should get $27,920

Table 5.4

I. Symbols:
  PV = Present value, what future cash flows are worth today
  FV_t = Future value, what cash flows are worth in the future
    r = Interest rate, rate of return, or discount rate per period—typically, but not always, one year
    t = Number of periods—typically, but not always, the number of years
    C = Cash amount

II. Future value of C invested at r percent for t periods:
  $FV_t = C \times (1 + r)^t$
  The term $(1 + r)^t$ is called the *future value factor*.

III. Present value of C to be received in t periods at r percent per period:
  $PV = C/(1 + r)^t$
  The term $1/(1 + r)^t$ is called the *present value factor*.

IV. The basic present value equation giving the relationship between present and future value is:
  $PV = FV_t/(1 + r)^t$

Key Concepts and Skills

- Be able to compute the future value of multiple cash flows
- Be able to compute the present value of multiple cash flows
- Be able to compute loan payments
- Be able to find the interest rate on a loan
- Understand how loans are amortized or paid off
- Understand how interest rates are quoted

Chapter Outline

- Future and Present Values of Multiple Cash Flows
- Valuing Level Cash Flows: Annuities and Perpetuities
- Comparing Rates: The Effect of Compounding Periods
- Loan Types and Loan Amortization

6.3 Multiple Cash Flows – Future Value Example 6.1

- Find the value at year 3 of each cash flow and add them together.
  - Today (year 0): FV = $7000(1.08)^3$ = 8,817.98
  - Year 1: FV = $4,000(1.08)^2$ = 4,665.60
  - Year 2: FV = $4,000(1.08)$ = 4,320
  - Year 3: value = 4,000
  - Total value in 3 years = 8817.98 + 4665.60 + 4320 + 4000 = 21,803.58
- Value at year 4 = 21,803.58(1.08) = 23,547.87

6.4 Multiple Cash Flows – FV Example 2

- Suppose you invest $500 in a mutual fund today and $600 in one year. If the fund pays 9% annually, how much will you have in two years?
  - FV = $500(1.09)^2 + 600(1.09)$ = 1248.05

6.5 Multiple Cash Flows – Example 2 Continued

- How much will you have in 5 years if you make no further deposits?
- First way:
  - $FV = 500(1.09)^5 + 600(1.09)^4 = 1616.26$
- Second way – use value at year 2:
  - $FV = 1248.05(1.09)^3 = 1616.26$

6.6 Multiple Cash Flows – FV Example 3

- Suppose you plan to deposit $100 into an account in one year and $300 into the account in three years. How much will be in the account in five years if the interest rate is 8%?
  - $FV = 100(1.08)^4 + 300(1.08)^2 = 136.05 + 349.92 = 485.97$

6.7 Multiple Cash Flows – Present Value Example 6.3

- Find the PV of each cash flows and add them
  - Year 1 CF: $200 / (1.12)^1 = 178.57$
  - Year 2 CF: $400 / (1.12)^2 = 318.88$
  - Year 3 CF: $600 / (1.12)^3 = 427.07$
  - Year 4 CF: $800 / (1.12)^4 = 508.41$
  - Total PV = 178.57 + 318.88 + 427.07 + 508.41 = 1432.93

6.8 Example 6.3 Timeline

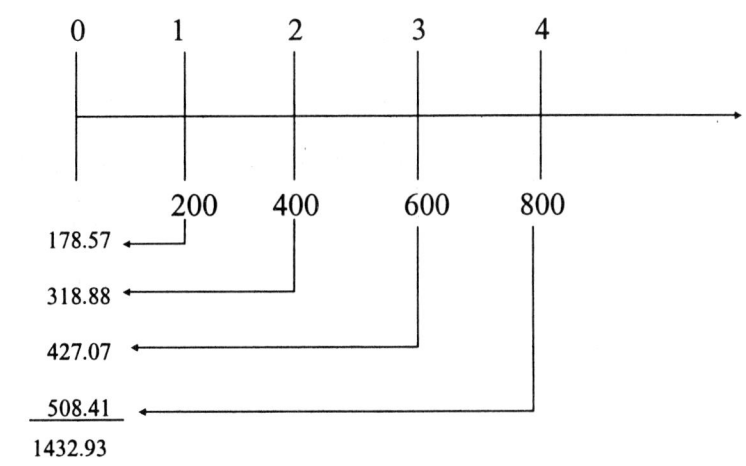

6.9 Multiple Cash Flows Using a Spreadsheet

- You can use the PV or FV functions in Excel to find the present value or future value of a set of cash flows
- Setting the data up is half the battle – if it is set up properly, then you can just copy the formulas
- Click on the Excel icon for an example

6.10 Multiple Cash Flows – PV Another Example

- You are considering an investment that will pay you $1000 in one year, $2000 in two years and $3000 in three years. If you want to earn 10% on your money, how much would you be willing to pay?
  - PV = $1000 / (1.1)^1 = 909.09$
  - PV = $2000 / (1.1)^2 = 1652.89$
  - PV = $3000 / (1.1)^3 = 2253.94$
  - PV = 909.09 + 1652.89 + 2253.94 = 4815.93

6.11 Multiple Uneven Cash Flows – Using the Calculator

- Another way to use the financial calculator for uneven cash flows is to use the cash flow keys
  - Texas Instruments BA-II Plus
    - Press CF and enter the cash flows beginning with year 0.
    - You have to press the "Enter" key for each cash flow
    - Use the down arrow key to move to the next cash flow
    - The "F" is the number of times a given cash flow occurs in consecutive years
    - Use the NPV key to compute the present value by entering the interest rate for I, pressing the down arrow and then compute
    - Clear the cash flow keys by pressing CF and then CLR Work

6.12 Decisions, Decisions

- Your broker calls you and tells you that he has this great investment opportunity. If you invest $100 today, you will receive $40 in one year and $75 in two years. If you require a 15% return on investments of this risk, should you take the investment?
  - Use the CF keys to compute the value of the investment
    - CF; $CF_0 = 0$; C01 = 40; F01 = 1; C02 = 75; F02 = 1
    - NPV; I = 15; CPT NPV = 91.49
  - No – the broker is charging more than you would be willing to pay.

6.13 Saving For Retirement

- You are offered the opportunity to put some money away for retirement. You will receive five annual payments of $25,000 each beginning in 40 years. How much would you be willing to invest today if you desire an interest rate of 12%?
  - Use cash flow keys:
    - CF; $CF_0 = 0$; C01 = 0; F01 = 39; C02 = 25000; F02 = 5; NPV; I = 12; CPT NPV = 1084.71

6.14 Saving For Retirement Timeline

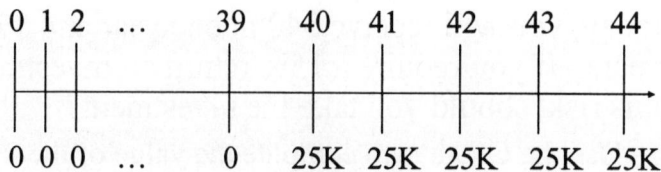

Notice that the year 0 cash flow = 0 ($CF_0 = 0$)

The cash flows years 1 – 39 are 0 (C01 = 0; F01 = 39)

The cash flows years 40 – 44 are 25,000 (C02 = 25,000; F02 = 5)

Quick Quiz – Part I

- Suppose you are looking at the following possible cash flows: Year 1 CF = $100; Years 2 and 3 CFs = $200; Years 4 and 5 CFs = $300. The required discount rate is 7%
- What is the value of the cash flows at year 5?
- What is the value of the cash flows today?
- What is the value of the cash flows at year 3?

Annuities and Perpetuities Defined

- Annuity – finite series of equal payments that occur at regular intervals
  - If the first payment occurs at the end of the period, it is called an ordinary annuity
  - If the first payment occurs at the beginning of the period, it is called an annuity due
- Perpetuity – infinite series of equal payments

Annuities and Perpetuities – Basic Formulas

- Perpetuity: PV = C / r
- Annuities:

$$PV = C \left[\frac{1 - \frac{1}{(1+r)^t}}{r} \right]$$

$$FV = C \left[\frac{(1+r)^t - 1}{r} \right]$$

Annuities and the Calculator

- You can use the PMT key on the calculator for the equal payment
- The sign convention still holds
- Ordinary annuity versus annuity due
    - You can switch your calculator between the two types by using the 2nd BGN 2nd Set on the TI BA-II Plus
    - If you see "BGN" or "Begin" in the display of your calculator, you have it set for an annuity due
    - Most problems are ordinary annuities

6.19 Annuity – Example 6.5

- You borrow money TODAY so you need to compute the present value.
    - 48 N; 1 I/Y; -632 PMT; CPT PV = 23,999.54 ($24,000)
- Formula:

$$PV = 632\left[\frac{1-\frac{1}{(1.01)^{48}}}{.01}\right] = 23,999.54$$

6.20 Annuity – Sweepstakes Example

- Suppose you win the Publishers Clearinghouse $10 million sweepstakes. The money is paid in equal annual installments of $333,333.33 over 30 years. If the appropriate discount rate is 5%, how much is the sweepstakes actually worth today?
    - PV = 333,333.33[1 – 1/1.05^{30}] / .05 = 5,124,150.29

6.21 Buying a House

- You are ready to buy a house and you have $20,000 for a down payment and closing costs. Closing costs are estimated to be 4% of the loan value. You have an annual salary of $36,000 and the bank is willing to allow your monthly mortgage payment to be equal to 28% of your monthly income. The interest rate on the loan is 6% per year with monthly compounding (.5% per month) for a 30-year fixed rate loan. How much money will the bank loan you? How much can you offer for the house?

6.22 Buying a House - Continued

- Bank loan
    - Monthly income = 36,000 / 12 = 3,000
    - Maximum payment = .28(3,000) = 840
    - PV = $840[1 - 1/1.005^{360}] / .005 = 140,105$
- Total Price
    - Closing costs = .04(140,105) = 5,604
    - Down payment = 20,000 − 5604 = 14,396
    - Total Price = 140,105 + 14,396 = 154,501

6.23 Annuities on the Spreadsheet - Example

- The present value and future value formulas in a spreadsheet include a place for annuity payments
- Click on the Excel icon to see an example

6.24 Quick Quiz – Part II

- You know the payment amount for a loan and you want to know how much was borrowed. Do you compute a present value or a future value?
- You want to receive 5000 per month in retirement. If you can earn .75% per month and you expect to need the income for 25 years, how much do you need to have in your account at retirement?

6.25 Finding the Payment

- Suppose you want to borrow $20,000 for a new car. You can borrow at 8% per year, compounded monthly (8/12 = .66667% per month). If you take a 4 year loan, what is your monthly payment?
    - $20{,}000 = C[1 - 1 / 1.0066667^{48}] / .0066667$
    - $C = 488.26$

6.26 Finding the Payment on a Spreadsheet

- Another TVM formula that can be found in a spreadsheet is the payment formula
    - PMT(rate,nper,pv,fv)
    - The same sign convention holds as for the PV and FV formulas
- Click on the Excel icon for an example

Finding the Number of Payments – Example 6.6

- Start with the equation and remember your logs.
  - $1000 = 20(1 - 1/1.015^t) / .015$
  - $.75 = 1 - 1 / 1.015^t$
  - $1 / 1.015^t = .25$
  - $1 / .25 = 1.015^t$
  - $t = \ln(1/.25) / \ln(1.015) = 93.111$ months $= 7.75$ years
- And this is only if you don't charge anything more on the card!

Finding the Number of Payments – Another Example

- Suppose you borrow $2000 at 5% and you are going to make annual payments of $734.42. How long before you pay off the loan?
  - $2000 = 734.42(1 - 1/1.05^t) / .05$
  - $.136161869 = 1 - 1/1.05^t$
  - $1/1.05^t = .863838131$
  - $1.157624287 = 1.05^t$
  - $t = \ln(1.157624287) / \ln(1.05) = 3$ years

6.29 Finding the Rate

- Suppose you borrow $10,000 from your parents to buy a car. You agree to pay $207.58 per month for 60 months. What is the monthly interest rate?
  - Sign convention matters!!!
  - 60 N
  - 10,000 PV
  - -207.58 PMT
  - CPT I/Y = .75%

6.30 Annuity – Finding the Rate Without a Financial Calculator

- Trial and Error Process
  - Choose an interest rate and compute the PV of the payments based on this rate
  - Compare the computed PV with the actual loan amount
  - If the computed PV > loan amount, then the interest rate is too low
  - If the computed PV < loan amount, then the interest rate is too high
  - Adjust the rate and repeat the process until the computed PV and the loan amount are equal

Quick Quiz – Part III

- You want to receive $5000 per month for the next 5 years. How much would you need to deposit today if you can earn .75% per month?
- What monthly rate would you need to earn if you only have $200,000 to deposit?
- Suppose you have $200,000 to deposit and can earn .75% per month.
  - How many months could you receive the $5000 payment?
  - How much could you receive every month for 5 years?

Future Values for Annuities

- Suppose you begin saving for your retirement by depositing $2000 per year in an IRA. If the interest rate is 7.5%, how much will you have in 40 years?
  - FV = $2000(1.075^{40} - 1)/.075 = 454{,}513.04$

Annuity Due

- You are saving for a new house and you put $10,000 per year in an account paying 8%. The first payment is made today. How much will you have at the end of 3 years?
  - FV = 10,000[(1.08^3 − 1) / .08](1.08) = 35,061.12

Annuity Due Timeline

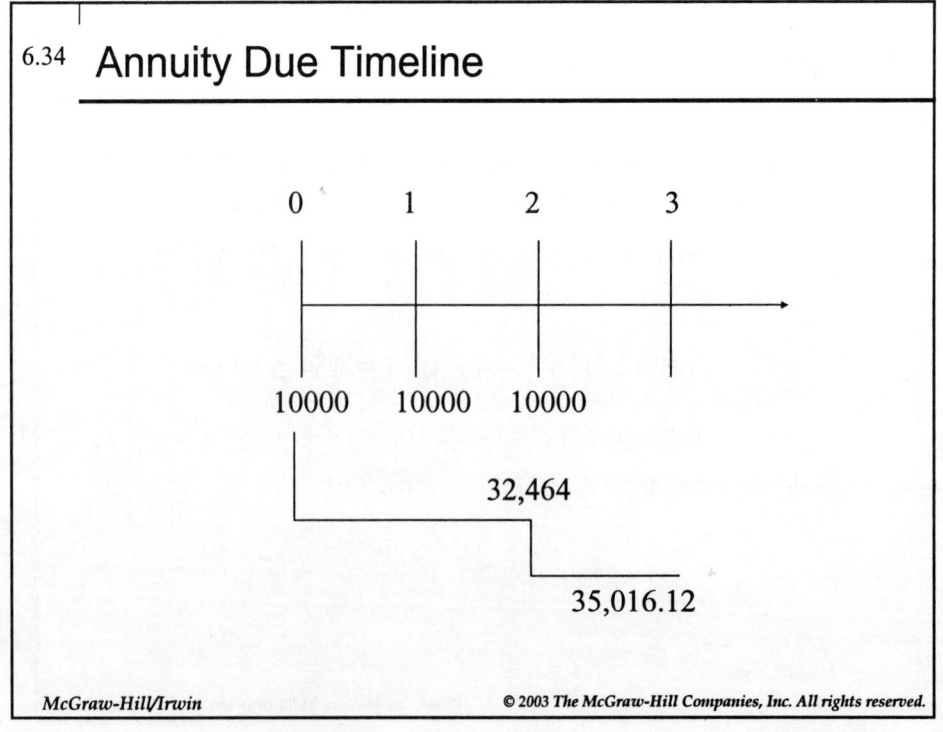

Perpetuity – Example 6.7

- Perpetuity formula: PV = C / r
- Current required return:
  - 40 = 1 / r
  - r = .025 or 2.5% per quarter
- Dividend for new preferred:
  - 100 = C / .025
  - C = 2.50 per quarter

Quick Quiz – Part IV

- You want to have $1 million to use for retirement in 35 years. If you can earn 1% per month, how much do you need to deposit on a monthly basis if the first payment is made in one month?
- What if the first payment is made today?
- You are considering preferred stock that pays a quarterly dividend of $1.50. If your desired return is 3% per quarter, how much would you be willing to pay?

6.37 Work the Web Example

- Another online financial calculator can be found at MoneyChimp
- Click on the web surfer and work the following example
  - Choose calculator and then annuity
  - You just inherited $5 million. If you can earn 6% on your money, how much can you withdraw each year for the next 40 years?
  - Datachimp assumes annuity due!!!
  - Payment = $313,497.81

6.38 Table 6.2

I. Symbols:
  PV = Present value, what future cash flows are worth today
  FV_t = Future value, what cash flows are worth in the future
  r = Interest rate, rate of return, or discount rate per period—typically, but not always, one year
  t = Number of periods—typically, but not always, the number of years
  C = Cash amount

II. Future value of C per period for t periods at r percent per period:
  $FV_t = C \times \{[(1 + r)^t - 1]/r\}$
  A series of identical cash flows is called an *annuity*, and the term $[(1 + r)^t - 1]/r$ is called the *annuity future value factor*.

III. Present value of C per period for t periods at r percent per period:
  $PV = C \times \{1 - [1/(1 + r)^t]\}/r$
  The term $\{1 - [1/(1 + r)^t]\}/r$ is called the *annuity present value factor*.

IV. Present value of a perpetuity of C per period:
  $PV = C/r$
  A *perpetuity* has the same cash flow every year forever.

6.39 Effective Annual Rate (EAR)

- This is the actual rate paid (or received) after accounting for compounding that occurs during the year
- If you want to compare two alternative investments with different compounding periods you need to compute the EAR and use that for comparison.

6.40 Annual Percentage Rate

- This is the annual rate that is quoted by law
- By definition APR = period rate times the number of periods per year
- Consequently, to get the period rate we rearrange the APR equation:
  - Period rate = APR / number of periods per year
- You should NEVER divide the effective rate by the number of periods per year – it will NOT give you the period rate

6.41 Computing APRs

- What is the APR if the monthly rate is .5%?
  - .5(12) = 6%
- What is the APR if the semiannual rate is .5%?
  - .5(2) = 1%
- What is the monthly rate if the APR is 12% with monthly compounding?
  - 12 / 12 = 1%
  - Can you divide the above APR by 2 to get the semiannual rate? NO!!! You need an APR based on semiannual compounding to find the semiannual rate.

6.42 Things to Remember

- You ALWAYS need to make sure that the interest rate and the time period match.
  - If you are looking at annual periods, you need an annual rate.
  - If you are looking at monthly periods, you need a monthly rate.
- If you have an APR based on monthly compounding, you have to use monthly periods for lump sums, or adjust the interest rate appropriately if you have payments other than monthly

6.43 Computing EARs - Example

- Suppose you can earn 1% per month on $1 invested today.
  - What is the APR? 1(12) = 12%
  - How much are you effectively earning?
    - FV = $1(1.01)^{12}$ = 1.1268
    - Rate = (1.1268 – 1) / 1 = .1268 = 12.68%
- Suppose if you put it in another account, you earn 3% per quarter.
  - What is the APR? 3(4) = 12%
  - How much are you effectively earning?
    - FV = $1(1.03)^4$ = 1.1255
    - Rate = (1.1255 – 1) / 1 = .1255 = 12.55%

6.44 EAR - Formula

$$EAR = \left[1 + \frac{APR}{m}\right]^m - 1$$

Remember that the APR is the quoted rate

6.45 Decisions, Decisions II

- You are looking at two savings accounts. One pays 5.25%, with daily compounding. The other pays 5.3% with semiannual compounding. Which account should you use?
  - First account:
    - EAR = $(1 + .0525/365)^{365} - 1 = 5.39\%$
  - Second account:
    - EAR = $(1 + .053/2)^2 - 1 = 5.37\%$
- Which account should you choose and why?

6.46 Decisions, Decisions II Continued

- Let's verify the choice. Suppose you invest $100 in each account. How much will you have in each account in one year?
  - First Account:
    - Daily rate = .0525 / 365 = .00014383562
    - FV = $100(1.00014383562)^{365} = 105.39$
  - Second Account:
    - Semiannual rate = .0539 / 2 = .0265
    - FV = $100(1.0265)^2 = 105.37$
- You have more money in the first account.

6.47 Computing APRs from EARs

- If you have an effective rate, how can you compute the APR? Rearrange the EAR equation and you get:

$$APR = m\left[(1 + EAR)^{1/m} - 1\right]$$

6.48 APR - Example

- Suppose you want to earn an effective rate of 12% and you are looking at an account that compounds on a monthly basis. What APR must they pay?

$$APR = 12\left[(1+.12)^{12} - 1\right] = .1138655152$$
or 11.39%

6.49 Computing Payments with APRs

- Suppose you want to buy a new computer system and the store is willing to sell it to allow you to make monthly payments. The entire computer system costs $3500. The loan period is for 2 years and the interest rate is 16.9% with monthly compounding. What is your monthly payment?
  - Monthly rate = .169 / 12 = .01408333333
  - Number of months = 2(12) = 24
  - $3500 = C[1 - 1 / 1.01408333333)^{24}] / .01408333333$
  - C = 172.88

6.50 Future Values with Monthly Compounding

- Suppose you deposit $50 a month into an account that has an APR of 9%, based on monthly compounding. How much will you have in the account in 35 years?
  - Monthly rate = .09 / 12 = .0075
  - Number of months = 35(12) = 420
  - $FV = 50[1.0075^{420} - 1] / .0075 = 147{,}089.22$

6.51 Present Value with Daily Compounding

- You need $15,000 in 3 years for a new car. If you can deposit money into an account that pays an APR of 5.5% based on daily compounding, how much would you need to deposit?
  - Daily rate = .055 / 365 = .00015068493
  - Number of days = 3(365) = 1095
  - FV = 15,000 / (1.00015068493)^{1095} = 12,718.56

6.52 Continuous Compounding

- Sometimes investments or loans are figured based on continuous compounding
- EAR = $e^q - 1$
  - The e is a special function on the calculator normally denoted by e^x
- Example: What is the effective annual rate of 7% compounded continuously?
  - EAR = $e^{.07} - 1$ = .0725 or 7.25%

6.53 Quick Quiz – Part V

- What is the definition of an APR?
- What is the effective annual rate?
- Which rate should you use to compare alternative investments or loans?
- Which rate do you need to use in the time value of money calculations?

6.54 Pure Discount Loans – Example 6.12

- Treasury bills are excellent examples of pure discount loans. The principal amount is repaid at some future date, without any periodic interest payments.
- If a T-bill promises to repay $10,000 in 12 months and the market interest rate is 7 percent, how much will the bill sell for in the market?
  - PV = 10,000 / 1.07 = 9345.79

6.55 Interest Only Loan - Example

- Consider a 5-year, interest only loan with a 7% interest rate. The principal amount is $10,000. Interest is paid annually.
  - What would the stream of cash flows be?
    - Years 1 – 4: Interest payments of .07(10,000) = 700
    - Year 5: Interest + principal = 10,700
- This cash flow stream is similar to the cash flows on corporate bonds and we will talk about them in greater detail later.

6.56 Amortized Loan with Fixed Principal Payment - Example

- Consider a $50,000, 10 year loan at 8% interest. The loan agreement requires the firm to pay $5,000 in principal each year plus interest for that year.
- Click on the Excel icon to see the amortization table

6.57 Amortized Loan with Fixed Payment - Example

- Each payment covers the interest expense plus reduces principal
- Consider a 4 year loan with annual payments. The interest rate is 8% and the principal amount is $5000.
  - What is the annual payment?
    - 4 N
    - 8 I/Y
    - 5000 PV
    - CPT PMT = -1509.60
- Click on the Excel icon to see the amortization table

6.58 Work the Web Example

- There are web sites available that can easily prepare amortization tables
- Click on the web surfer to check out the CMB Mortgage site and work the following example
- You have a loan of $25,000 and will repay the loan over 5 years at 8% interest.
  - What is your loan payment?
  - What does the amortization schedule look like?

Quick Quiz – Part VI

- What is a pure discount loan? What is a good example of a pure discount loan?
- What is an interest only loan? What is a good example of an interest only loan?
- What is an amortized loan? What is a good example of an amortized loan?

7.1 Key Concepts and Skills

- Know the important bond features and bond types
- Understand bond values and why they fluctuate
- Understand bond ratings and what they mean
- Understand the impact of inflation on interest rates
- Understand the term structure of interest rates and the determinants of bond yields

7.2 Chapter Outline

- Bonds and Bond Valuation
- More on Bond Features
- Bond Ratings
- Some Different Types of Bonds
- Bond Markets
- Inflation and Interest Rates
- Determinants of Bond Yields

7.3 Bond Definitions

- Bond
- Par value (face value)
- Coupon rate
- Coupon payment
- Maturity date
- Yield or Yield to maturity

7.4 Present Value of Cash Flows as Rates Change

- Bond Value = PV of coupons + PV of par
- Bond Value = PV annuity + PV of lump sum
- Remember, as interest rates increase the PV's decrease
- So, as interest rates increase, bond prices decrease and vice versa

7.5 Valuing a Discount Bond with Annual Coupons

- Consider a bond with a coupon rate of 10% and coupons paid annually. The par value is $1000 and the bond has 5 years to maturity. The yield to maturity is 11%. What is the value of the bond?
  - Using the formula:
    - B = PV of annuity + PV of lump sum
    - $B = 100[1 - 1/(1.11)^5] / .11 + 1000 / (1.11)^5$
    - B = 369.59 + 593.45 = 963.04
  - Using the calculator:
    - N = 5; I/Y = 11; PMT = 100; FV = 1000
    - CPT PV = -963.04

7.6 Valuing a Premium Bond with Annual Coupons

- Suppose you are looking at a bond that has a 10% annual coupon and a face value of $1000. There are 20 years to maturity and the yield to maturity is 8%. What is the price of this bond?
  - Using the formula:
    - B = PV of annuity + PV of lump sum
    - $B = 100[1 - 1/(1.08)^{20}] / .08 + 1000 / (1.08)^{20}$
    - B = 981.81 + 214.55 = 1196.36
  - Using the calculator:
    - N = 20; I/Y = 8; PMT = 100; FV = 1000
    - CPT PV = -1196.36

7.7 Graphical Relationship Between Price and Yield-to-maturity

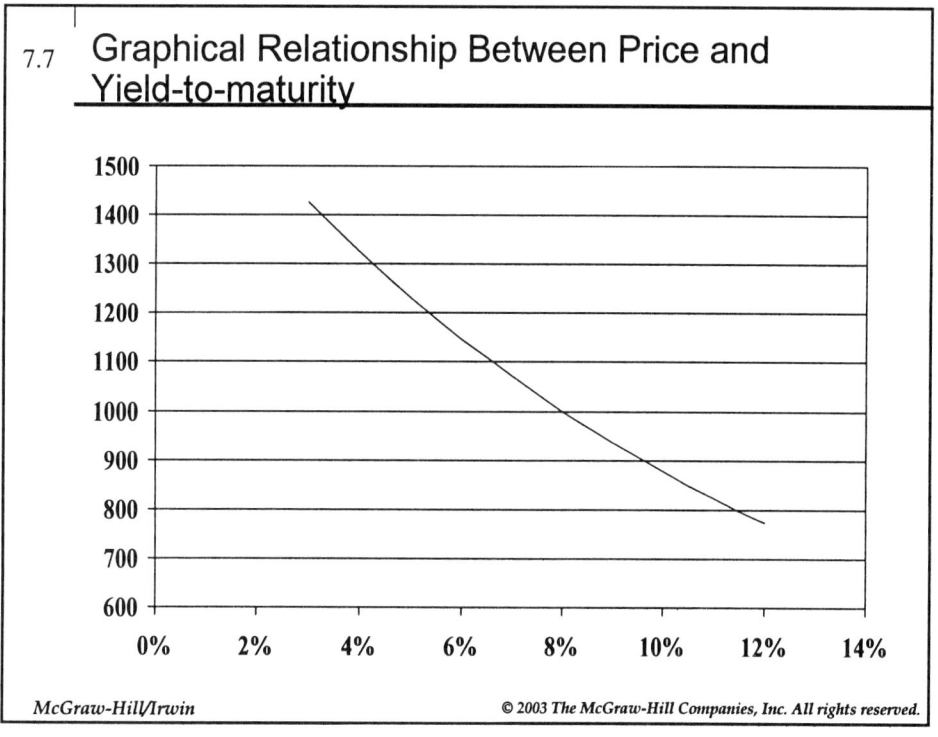

7.8 Bond Prices: Relationship Between Coupon and Yield

- If YTM = coupon rate, then par value = bond price
- If YTM > coupon rate, then par value > bond price
  - Why?
  - Selling at a discount, called a discount bond
- If YTM < coupon rate, then par value < bond price
  - Why?
  - Selling at a premium, called a premium bond

7.9 The Bond-Pricing Equation

$$\text{Bond Value} = C\left[\frac{1-\dfrac{1}{(1+r)^t}}{r}\right] + \frac{F}{(1+r)^t}$$

7.10 Example 7.1

- Find present values based on the payment period
    - How many coupon payments are there?
    - What is the semiannual coupon payment?
    - What is the semiannual yield?
    - $B = 70[1 - 1/(1.08)^{14}] / .08 + 1000 / (1.08)^{14} = 917.56$
    - Or PMT = 70; N = 14; I/Y = 8; FV = 1000; CPT PV = -917.56

Interest Rate Risk

- Price Risk
  - Change in price due to changes in interest rates
  - Long-term bonds have more price risk than short-term bonds
- Reinvestment Rate Risk
  - Uncertainty concerning rates at which cash flows can be reinvested
  - Short-term bonds have more reinvestment rate risk than long-term bonds

Figure 7.2

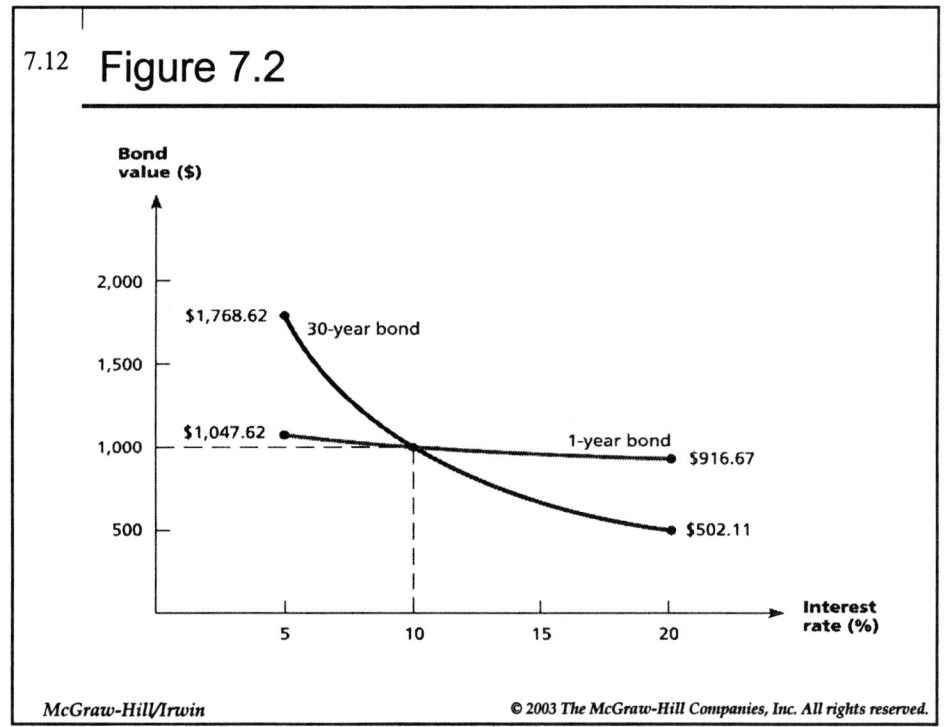

7.13 Computing Yield-to-maturity

- Yield-to-maturity is the rate implied by the current bond price
- Finding the YTM requires trial and error if you do not have a financial calculator and is similar to the process for finding r with an annuity
- If you have a financial calculator, enter N, PV, PMT and FV, remembering the sign convention (PMT and FV need to have the same sign, PV the opposite sign)

7.14 YTM with Annual Coupons

- Consider a bond with a 10% annual coupon rate, 15 years to maturity and a par value of $1000. The current price is $928.09.
  - Will the yield be more or less than 10%?
  - N = 15; PV = -928.09; FV = 1000; PMT = 100
  - CPT I/Y = 11%

7.15 YTM with Semiannual Coupons

- Suppose a bond with a 10% coupon rate and semiannual coupons, has a face value of $1000, 20 years to maturity and is selling for $1197.93.
  - Is the YTM more or less than 10%?
  - What is the semiannual coupon payment?
  - How many periods are there?
  - N = 40; PV = -1197.93; PMT = 50; FV = 1000; CPT I/Y = 4% (Is this the YTM?)
  - YTM = 4%*2 = 8%

7.16 Table 7.1

I. Finding the value of a bond

$$\text{Bond value} = C \times [1 - 1/(1 + r)^t]/r + F/(1 + r)^t$$

where
- C = Coupon paid each period
- r = Rate per period
- t = Number of periods
- F = Bond's face value

II. Finding the yield on a bond

Given a bond value, coupon, time to maturity, and face value, it is possible to find the implicit discount rate, or yield to maturity, by trial and error only. To do this, try different discount rates until the calculated bond value equals the given value (or let a financial calculator do it for you). Remember that increasing the rate decreases the bond value.

7.17 Bond Pricing Theorems

- Bonds of similar risk (and maturity) will be priced to yield about the same return, regardless of the coupon rate
- If you know the price of one bond, you can estimate its YTM and use that to find the price of the second bond
- This is a useful concept that can be transferred to valuing assets other than bonds

7.18 Bond Prices with a Spreadsheet

- There is a specific formula for finding bond prices on a spreadsheet
    - PRICE(Settlement,Maturity,Rate,Yld,Redemption, Frequency,Basis)
    - YIELD(Settlement,Maturity,Rate,Pr,Redemption, Frequency,Basis)
    - Settlement and maturity need to be actual dates
    - The redemption and Pr need to given as % of par value
- Click on the Excel icon for an example

7.19 Differences Between Debt and Equity

- Debt
  - Not an ownership interest
  - Creditors do not have voting rights
  - Interest is considered a cost of doing business and is tax deductible
  - Creditors have legal recourse if interest or principal payments are missed
  - Excess debt can lead to financial distress and bankruptcy

- Equity
  - Ownership interest
  - Common stockholders vote for the board of directors and other issues
  - Dividends are not considered a cost of doing business and are not tax deductible
  - Dividends are not a liability of the firm and stockholders have no legal recourse if dividends are not paid
  - An all equity firm can not go bankrupt

7.20 The Bond Indenture

- Contract between the company and the bondholders and includes
  - The basic terms of the bonds
  - The total amount of bonds issued
  - A description of property used as security, if applicable
  - Sinking fund provisions
  - Call provisions
  - Details of protective covenants

Bond Classifications

- Registered vs. Bearer Forms
- Security
  - Collateral – secured by financial securities
  - Mortgage – secured by real property, normally land or buildings
  - Debentures – unsecured
  - Notes – unsecured debt with original maturity less than 10 years
- Seniority

Bond Characteristics and Required Returns

- The coupon rate depends on the risk characteristics of the bond when issued
- Which bonds will have the higher coupon, all else equal?
  - Secured debt versus a debenture
  - Subordinated debenture versus senior debt
  - A bond with a sinking fund versus one without
  - A callable bond versus a non-callable bond

7.23 Bond Ratings – Investment Quality

- High Grade
  - Moody's Aaa and S&P AAA – capacity to pay is extremely strong
  - Moody's Aa and S&P AA – capacity to pay is very strong
- Medium Grade
  - Moody's A and S&P A – capacity to pay is strong, but more susceptible to changes in circumstances
  - Moody's Baa and S&P BBB – capacity to pay is adequate, adverse conditions will have more impact on the firm's ability to pay

7.24 Bond Ratings - Speculative

- Low Grade
  - Moody's Ba, B, Caa and Ca
  - S&P BB, B, CCC, CC
  - Considered speculative with respect to capacity to pay. The "B" ratings are the lowest degree of speculation.
- Very Low Grade
  - Moody's C and S&P C – income bonds with no interest being paid
  - Moody's D and S&P D – in default with principal and interest in arrears

Government Bonds

- Treasury Securities
  - Federal government debt
  - T-bills – pure discount bonds with original maturity of one year or less
  - T-notes – coupon debt with original maturity between one and ten years
  - T-bonds coupon debt with original maturity greater than ten years
- Municipal Securities
  - Debt of state and local governments
  - Varying degrees of default risk, rated similar to corporate debt
  - Interest received is tax-exempt at the federal level

Example 7.3

- A taxable bond has a yield of 8% and a municipal bond has a yield of 6%
  - If you are in a 40% tax bracket, which bond do you prefer?
    - 8%(1 - .4) = 4.8%
    - The after-tax return on the corporate bond is 4.8%, compared to a 6% return on the municipal
  - At what tax rate would you be indifferent between the two bonds?
    - 8%(1 – T) = 6%
    - T = 25%

7.27 Zero-Coupon Bonds

- Make no periodic interest payments (coupon rate = 0%)
- The entire yield-to-maturity comes from the difference between the purchase price and the par value
- Cannot sell for more than par value
- Sometimes called zeroes, or deep discount bonds
- Treasury Bills and principal only Treasury strips are good examples of zeroes

7.28 Floating Rate Bonds

- Coupon rate floats depending on some index value
- Examples – adjustable rate mortgages and inflation-linked Treasuries
- There is less price risk with floating rate bonds
  - The coupon floats, so it is less likely to differ substantially from the yield-to-maturity
- Coupons may have a "collar" – the rate cannot go above a specified "ceiling" or below a specified "floor"

Other Bond Types

- Disaster bonds
- Income bonds
- Convertible bonds
- Put bond
- There are many other types of provisions that can be added to a bond and many bonds have several provisions – it is important to recognize how these provisions affect required returns

Bond Markets

- Primarily over-the-counter transactions with dealers connected electronically
- Extremely large number of bond issues, but generally low daily volume in single issues
- Makes getting up-to-date prices difficult, particularly on small company or municipal issues
- Treasury securities are an exception

7.31 Work the Web Example

- Bond quotes are available online
- One good site is Bonds Online
- Click on the web surfer to go to the site
  - Follow the bond search, corporate links
  - Choose a company, enter it under Express Search Issue and see what you can find!

7.32 Bond Quotations

- Highlighted quote in Figure 7.3
  - ATT 6s09   6.4   177   93 7/8   + ¼
  - What company are we looking at?
  - What is the coupon rate? If the bond has a $1000 face value, what is the coupon payment each year?
  - When does the bond mature?
  - What is the current yield? How is it computed?
  - How many bonds trade that day?
  - What is the quoted price?
  - How much did the price change from the previous day?

Treasury Quotations

- Highlighted quote in Figure 7.4
  - 8 Nov 21   125:05   125:11   -46   5.86
  - What is the coupon rate on the bond?
  - When does the bond mature?
  - What is the bid price? What does this mean?
  - What is the ask price? What does this mean?
  - How much did the price change from the previous day?
  - What is the yield based on the ask price?

Inflation and Interest Rates

- Real rate of interest – change in purchasing power
- Nominal rate of interest – quoted rate of interest, change in purchasing power and inflation
- The ex ante nominal rate of interest includes our desired real rate of return plus an adjustment for expected inflation

The Fisher Effect

- The Fisher Effect defines the relationship between real rates, nominal rates and inflation
- $(1 + R) = (1 + r)(1 + h)$, where
  - R = nominal rate
  - r = real rate
  - h = expected inflation rate
- Approximation
  - $R = r + h$

Example 7.6

- If we require a 10% real return and we expect inflation to be 8%, what is the nominal rate?
- $R = (1.1)(1.08) - 1 = .188 = 18.8\%$
- Approximation: $R = 10\% + 8\% = 18\%$
- Because the real return and expected inflation are relatively high, there is significant difference between the actual Fisher Effect and the approximation.

Term Structure of Interest Rates

- Term structure is the relationship between time to maturity and yields, all else equal
- It is important to recognize that we pull out the effect of default risk, different coupons, etc.
- Yield curve – graphical representation of the term structure
  - Normal – upward-sloping, long-term yields are higher than short-term yields
  - Inverted – downward-sloping, long-term yields are lower than short-term yields

Figure 7.6 – Upward-Sloping Yield Curve

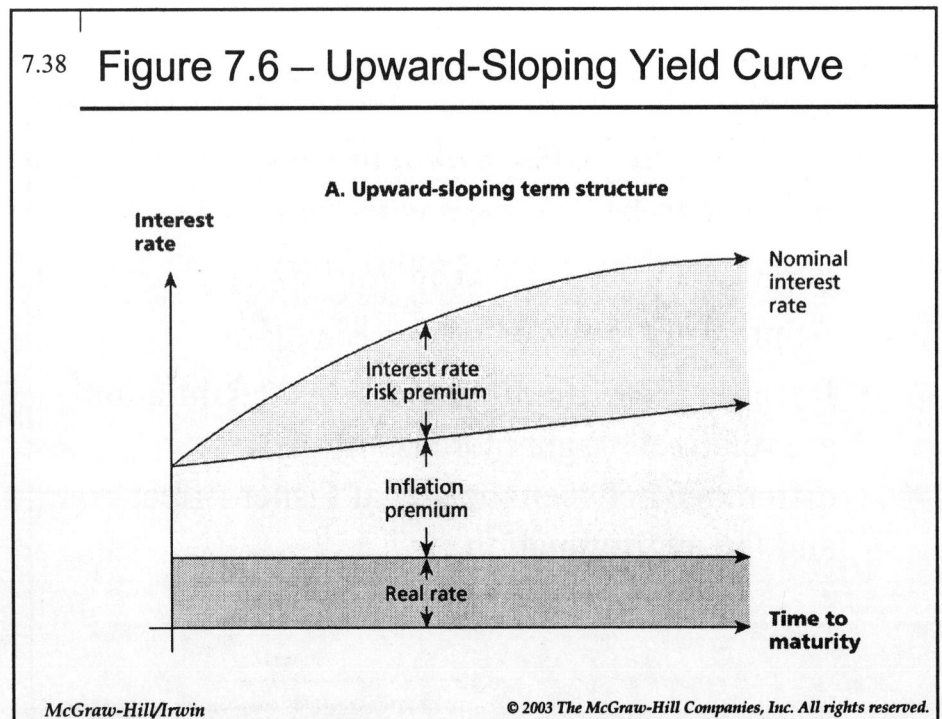

7.39 Figure 7.6 – Downward-Sloping Yield Curve

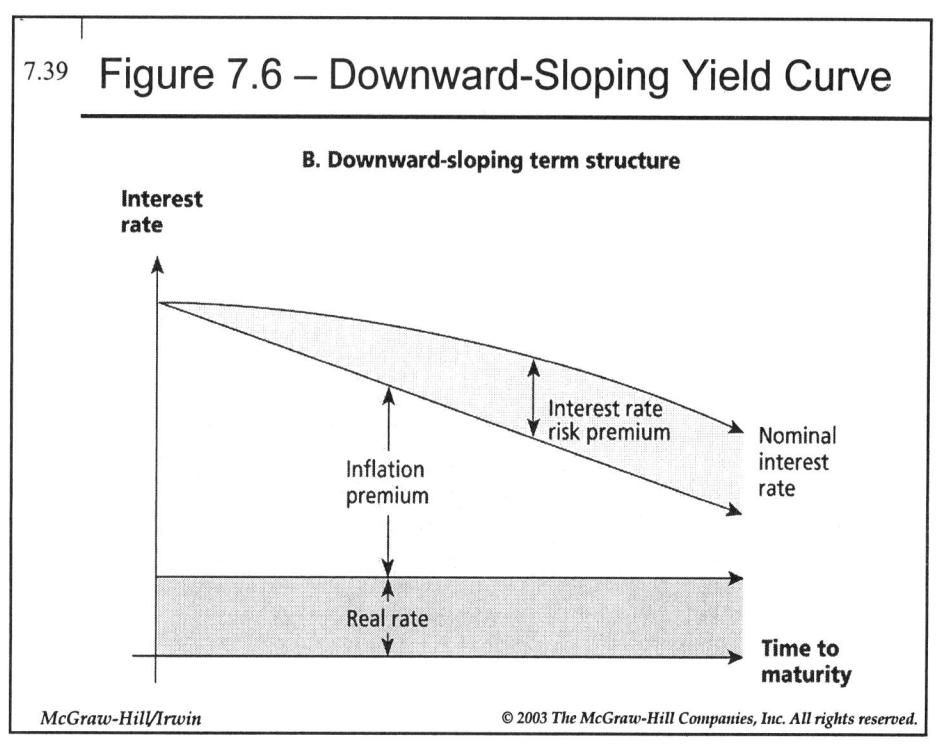

7.40 Figure 7.7 – Treasury Yield Curve May 11, 2001

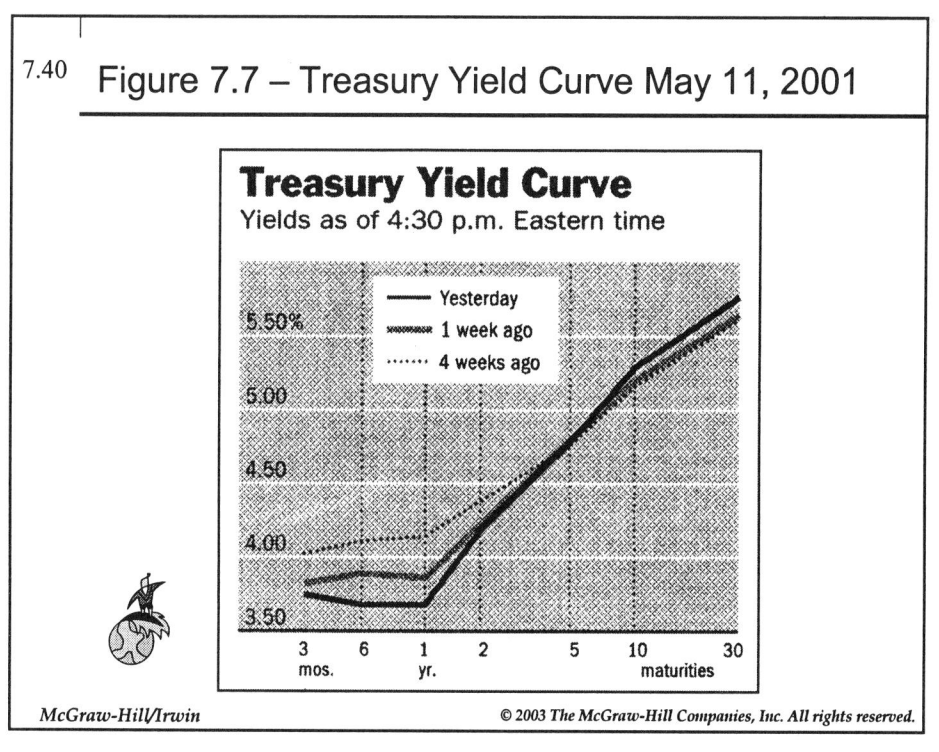

7.41 Factors Affecting Required Return

- Default risk premium – remember bond ratings
- Taxability premium – remember municipal versus taxable
- Liquidity premium – bonds that have more frequent trading will generally have lower required returns
- Anything else that affects the risk of the cash flows to the bondholders, will affect the required returns

7.42 Quick Quiz

- How do you find the value of a bond and why do bond prices change?
- What is a bond indenture and what are some of the important features?
- What are bond ratings and why are they important?
- How does inflation affect interest rates?
- What is the term structure of interest rates?
- What factors determine the required return on bonds?

8.1 Key Concepts and Skills

- Understand how stock prices depend on future dividends and dividend growth
- Be able to compute stock prices using the dividend growth model
- Understand how corporate directors are elected
- Understand how stock markets work
- Understand how stock prices are quoted

8.2 Chapter Outline

- Common Stock Valuation
- Some Features of Common and Preferred Stocks
- The Stock Markets

8.3 Cash Flows for Stockholders

- If you buy a share of stock, you can receive cash in two ways
  - The company pays dividends
  - You sell your shares, either to another investor in the market or back to the company
- As with bonds, the price of the stock is the present value of these expected cash flows

8.4 One Period Example

- Suppose you are thinking of purchasing the stock of Moore Oil, Inc. and you expect it to pay a $2 dividend in one year and you believe that you can sell the stock for $14 at that time. If you require a return of 20% on investments of this risk, what is the maximum you would be willing to pay?
  - Compute the PV of the expected cash flows
  - Price = (14 + 2) / (1.2) = $13.33
  - Or FV = 16; I/Y = 20; N = 1; CPT PV = -13.33

Two Period Example

- Now what if you decide to hold the stock for two years? In addition to the dividend in one year, you expect a dividend of $2.10 in and a stock price of $14.70 at the end of year 2. Now how much would you be willing to pay?
    - PV = 2 / (1.2) + (2.10 + 14.70) / (1.2)^2 = 13.33
    - Or CF_0 = 0; C01 = 2; F01 = 1; C02 = 16.80; F02 = 1; NPV; I = 20; CPT NPV = 13.33

Three Period Example

- Finally, what if you decide to hold the stock for three periods? In addition to the dividends at the end of years 1 and 2, you expect to receive a dividend of $2.205 at the end of year 3 and a stock price of $15.435. Now how much would you be willing to pay?
    - PV = 2 / 1.2 + 2.10 / (1.2)^2 + (2.205 + 15.435) / (1.2)^3 = 13.33
    - Or CF_0 = 0; C01 = 2; F01 = 1; C02 = 2.10; F02 = 1; C03 = 17.64; F03 = 1; NPV; I = 20; CPT NPV = 13.33

8.7 Developing The Model

- You could continue to push back when you would sell the stock
- You would find that the price of the stock is really just the *present value of <u>all</u> expected future dividends*
- So, how can we estimate all future dividend payments?

8.8 Estimating Dividends: Special Cases

- Constant dividend
  - The firm will pay a constant dividend forever
  - This is like preferred stock
  - The price is computed using the perpetuity formula
- Constant dividend growth
  - The firm will increase the dividend by a constant percent every period
- Supernormal growth
  - Dividend growth is not consistent initially, but settles down to constant growth eventually

8.9 Zero Growth

- If dividends are expected at regular intervals forever, then this is like preferred stock and is valued as a perpetuity
- $P_0 = D / R$
- Suppose stock is expected to pay a $0.50 dividend every quarter and the required return is 10% with quarterly compounding. What is the price?
  - $P_0 = .50 / (.1 / 4) = \$20$

8.10 Dividend Growth Model

- Dividends are expected to grow at a constant percent per period.
  - $P_0 = D_1/(1+R) + D_2/(1+R)^2 + D_3/(1+R)^3 + \ldots$
  - $P_0 = D_0(1+g)/(1+R) + D_0(1+g)^2/(1+R)^2 + D_0(1+g)^3/(1+R)^3 + \ldots$
- With a little algebra, this reduces to:

$$P_0 = \frac{D_0(1+g)}{R-g} = \frac{D_1}{R-g}$$

DGM – Example 1

- Suppose Big D, Inc. just paid a dividend of $.50. It is expected to increase its dividend by 2% per year. If the market requires a return of 15% on assets of this risk, how much should the stock be selling for?
- $P_0 = .50(1+.02) / (.15 - .02) = \$3.92$

DGM – Example 2

- Suppose TB Pirates, Inc. is expected to pay a $2 dividend in one year. If the dividend is expected to grow at 5% per year and the required return is 20%, what is the price?
  - $P_0 = 2 / (.2 - .05) = \$13.33$
  - Why isn't the $2 in the numerator multiplied by (1.05) in this example?

8.13 Stock Price Sensitivity to Dividend Growth, g

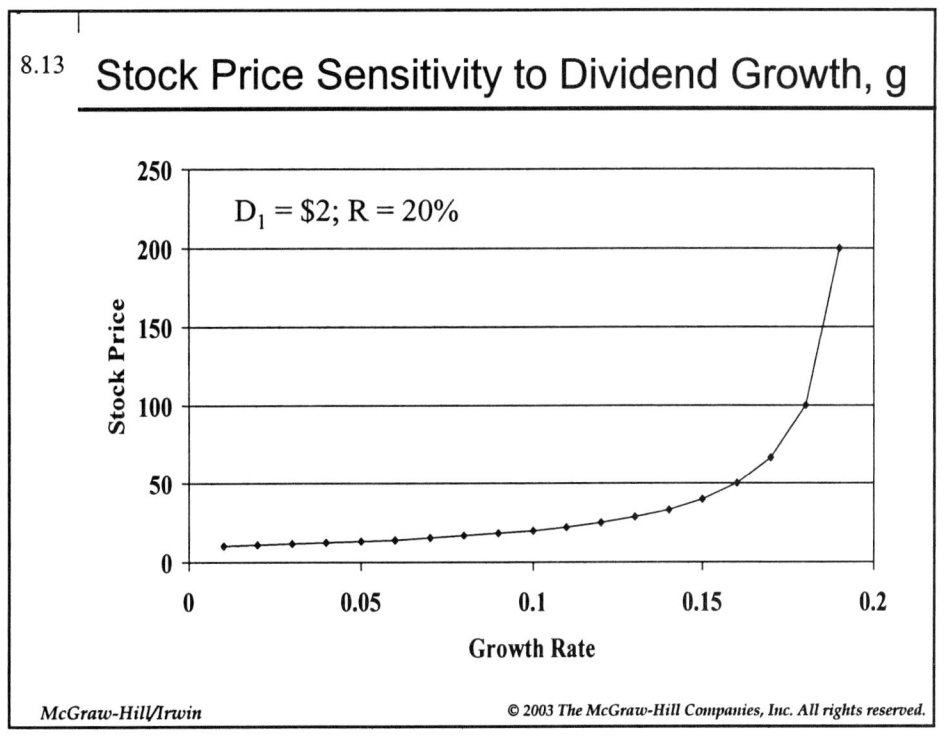

$D_1 = \$2;\ R = 20\%$

8.14 Stock Price Sensitivity to Required Return, R

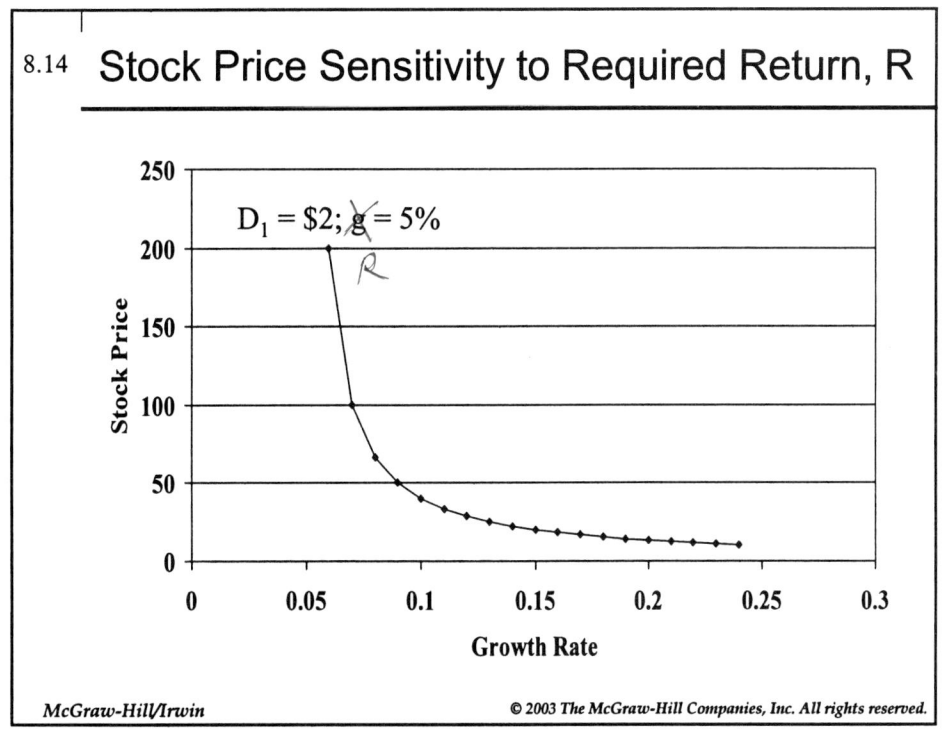

$D_1 = \$2;\ g = 5\%$

Example 8.3 Gordon Growth Company - I

- Gordon Growth Company is expected to pay a dividend of $4 next period and dividends are expected to grow at 6% per year. The required return is 16%.
- What is the current price?
    - $P_0 = 4 / (.16 - .06) = \$40$
    - Remember that we already have the dividend expected next year, so we don't multiply the dividend by $1+g$

Example 8.3 – Gordon Growth Company - II

- What is the price expected to be in year 4?
    - $P_4 = D_4(1 + g) / (R - g) = D_5 / (R - g)$
    - $P_4 = 4(1+.06)^4 / (.16 - .06) = 50.50$
- What is the implied return given the change in price during the four year period?
    - $50.50 = 40(1+\text{return})^4$; return = 6%
    - PV = -40; FV = 50.50; N = 4; CPT I/Y = 6%
- The price grows at the same rate as the dividends

8.17 Nonconstant Growth Problem Statement

- Suppose a firm is expected to increase dividends by 20% in one year and by 15% in two years. After that dividends will increase at a rate of 5% per year indefinitely. If the last dividend was $1 and the required return is 20%, what is the price of the stock?
- Remember that we have to find the PV of *all* expected future dividends.

8.18 Nonconstant Growth – Example Solution

- Compute the dividends until growth levels off
  - $D_1 = 1(1.2) = \$1.20$
  - $D_2 = 1.20(1.15) = \$1.38$
  - $D_3 = 1.38(1.05) = \$1.449$
- Find the expected future price
  - $P_2 = D_3 / (R - g) = 1.449 / (.2 - .05) = 9.66$
- Find the present value of the expected future cash flows
  - $P_0 = 1.20 / (1.2) + (1.38 + 9.66) / (1.2)^2 = 8.67$

8.19 Quick Quiz – Part I

- What is the value of a stock that is expected to pay a constant dividend of $2 per year if the required return is 15%?
- What if the company starts increasing dividends by 3% per year, beginning with the next dividend? The required return stays at 15%.

8.20 Using the DGM to Find R

- Start with the DGM:

$$P_0 = \frac{D_0(1+g)}{R-g} = \frac{D_1}{R-g}$$

rearrange and solve for R

$$R = \frac{D_0(1+g)}{P_0} + g = \frac{D_1}{P_0} + g$$

8.21 Finding the Required Return - Example

- Suppose a firm's stock is selling for $10.50. They just paid a $1 dividend and dividends are expected to grow at 5% per year. What is the required return?
  - R = [1(1.05)/10.50] + .05 = 15%
- What is the dividend yield?
  - 1(1.05) / 10.50 = 10%
- What is the capital gains yield?
  - g = 5%

8.22 Table 8.1 - Summary of Stock Valuation

I. The general case

In general, the price today of a share of stock, P_0, is the present value of all of its future dividends, $D_1, D_2, D_3, \ldots$:

$$P_0 = \frac{D_1}{(1+R)^1} + \frac{D_2}{(1+R)^2} + \frac{D_3}{(1+R)^3} + \cdots$$

where R is the required return.

II. Constant growth case

If the dividend grows at a steady rate, g, then the price can be written as:

$$P_0 = \frac{D_1}{R-g}$$

This result is called the *dividend growth model*.

III. Supernormal growth

If the dividend grows steadily after t periods, then the price can be written as:

$$P_0 = \frac{D_1}{(1+R)^1} + \frac{D_2}{(1+R)^2} + \cdots + \frac{D_t}{(1+R)^t} + \frac{P_t}{(1+R)^t}$$

where

$$P_t = \frac{D_t \times (1+g)}{(R-g)}$$

IV. The required return

The required return, R, can be written as the sum of two things:

$$R = D_1/P_0 + g$$

where D_1/P_0 is the *dividend yield* and g is the *capital gains yield* (which is the same thing as the growth rate in dividends for the steady growth case).

8.23 Feature of Common Stock

- Voting Rights
- Proxy voting
- Classes of stock
- Other Rights
  - Share proportionally in declared dividends
  - Share proportionally in remaining assets during liquidation
  - Preemptive right – first shot at new stock issue to maintain proportional ownership if desired

8.24 Dividend Characteristics

- Dividends are not a liability of the firm until a dividend has been declared by the Board
- Consequently, a firm cannot go bankrupt for not declaring dividends
- Dividends and Taxes
  - Dividend payments are not considered a business expense, therefore, they are not tax deductible
  - Dividends received by individuals are taxed as ordinary income
  - Dividends received by corporations have a minimum 70% exclusion from taxable income

Features of Preferred Stock

- Dividends
  - Stated dividend that must be paid before dividends can be paid to common stockholders
  - Dividends are not a liability of the firm and preferred dividends can be deferred indefinitely
  - Most preferred dividends are cumulative – any missed preferred dividends have to be paid before common dividends can be paid
- Preferred stock generally does not carry voting rights

Stock Market

- Dealers vs. Brokers
- New York Stock Exchange (NYSE)
  - Largest stock market in the world
  - Members
    - Own seats on the exchange
    - Commission brokers
    - Specialists
    - Floor brokers
    - Floor traders
  - Operations
  - Floor activity

8.27 NASDAQ

- Not a physical exchange – computer based quotation system
- Multiple market makers
- Electronic Communications Networks
- Three levels of information
  - Level 1 – median quotes, registered representatives
  - Level 2 – view quotes, brokers & dealers
  - Level 3 – view and update quotes, dealers only
- Large portion of technology stocks

8.28 Work the Web Example

- Electronic Communications Networks provide trading in NASDAQ securities
- The Island allows the public to view the "order book" in real time
- Click on the web surfer and visit The Island!

8.29 Reading Stock Quotes

- Sample Quote
  -3.3 33.25 20.75 Harris HRS   .20 .7 87 3358 29.60 +0.50
- What information is provided in the stock quote?
- Click on the web surfer to go to CNBC for current stock quotes.

8.30 Quick Quiz – Part II

- You observe a stock price of $18.75. You expect a dividend growth rate of 5% and the most recent dividend was $1.50. What is the required return? $\frac{1.50(1.05)}{18.75} + .05 = .134$
- What are some of the major characteristics of common stock?
- What are some of the major characteristics of preferred stock?

9.1 Key Concepts and Skills

- Be able to compute payback and discounted payback and understand their shortcomings
- Understand accounting rates of return and their shortcomings
- Be able to compute the internal rate of return and understand its strengths and weaknesses
- Be able to compute the net present value and understand why it is the best decision criterion

9.2 Chapter Outline

- Net Present Value
- The Payback Rule
- The Discounted Payback
- The Average Accounting Return
- The Internal Rate of Return
- The Profitability Index
- The Practice of Capital Budgeting

9.3 Good Decision Criteria

- We need to ask ourselves the following questions when evaluating decision criteria
  - Does the decision rule adjust for the time value of money?
  - Does the decision rule adjust for risk?
  - Does the decision rule provide information on whether we are creating value for the firm?

9.4 Project Example Information

- You are looking at a new project and you have estimated the following cash flows:
  - Year 0: CF = -165,000
  - Year 1: CF = 63,120; NI = 13,620
  - Year 2: CF = 70,800; NI = 3,300
  - Year 3: CF = 91,080; NI = 29,100
  - Average Book Value = 72,000
- Your required return for assets of this risk is 12%.

9.5 Net Present Value

- The difference between the market value of a project and its cost
- How much value is created from undertaking an investment?
  - The first step is to estimate the expected future cash flows.
  - The second step is to estimate the required return for projects of this risk level.
  - The third step is to find the present value of the cash flows and subtract the initial investment.

9.6 NPV – Decision Rule

- *If the NPV is positive, accept the project*
- A positive NPV means that the project is expected to add value to the firm and will therefore increase the wealth of the owners.
- Since our goal is to increase owner wealth, NPV is a direct measure of how well this project will meet our goal.

9.7 Computing NPV for the Project

- Using the formulas:
  - NPV = $63,120/(1.12) + 70,800/(1.12)^2 + 91,080/(1.12)^3 - 165,000 = 12,627.42$
- Using the calculator:
  - CF_0 = -165,000; C01 = 63,120; F01 = 1; C02 = 70,800; F02 = 1; C03 = 91,080; F03 = 1; NPV; I = 12; CPT NPV = 12,627.42
- *Do we accept or reject the project?*

9.8 Decision Criteria Test - NPV

- Does the NPV rule account for the time value of money?
- Does the NPV rule account for the risk of the cash flows?
- Does the NPV rule provide an indication about the increase in value?
- Should we consider the NPV rule for our primary decision criteria?

9.9 Calculating NPVs with a Spreadsheet

- Spreadsheets are an excellent way to compute NPVs, especially when you have to compute the cash flows as well.
- Using the NPV function
  - The first component is the required return entered as a decimal
  - The second component is the range of cash flows *beginning with year 1*
  - Subtract the initial investment after computing the NPV

9.10 Payback Period

- How long does it take to get the initial cost back in a nominal sense?
- Computation
  - Estimate the cash flows
  - Subtract the future cash flows from the initial cost until the initial investment has been recovered
- Decision Rule – *Accept if the payback period is less than some preset limit*

Computing Payback For The Project

- Assume we will accept the project if it pays back within two years.
  - Year 1: 165,000 – 63,120 = 101,880 still to recover
  - Year 2: 101,880 – 70,800 = 31,080 still to recover
  - Year 3: 31,080 – 91,080 = -60,000 *project pays back in year 3*
- ***Do we accept or reject the project?***

Decision Criteria Test - Payback

- Does the payback rule account for the time value of money?
- Does the payback rule account for the risk of the cash flows?
- Does the payback rule provide an indication about the increase in value?
- Should we consider the payback rule for our primary decision criteria?

9.13 Advantages and Disadvantages of Payback

- Advantages
  - Easy to understand
  - Adjusts for uncertainty of later cash flows
  - Biased towards liquidity
- Disadvantages
  - Ignores the time value of money
  - Requires an arbitrary cutoff point
  - Ignores cash flows beyond the cutoff date
  - Biased against long-term projects, such as research and development, and new projects

9.14 Discounted Payback Period

- Compute the present value of each cash flow and then determine how long it takes to payback on a discounted basis
- Compare to a specified required period
- Decision Rule - *Accept the project if it pays back on a discounted basis within the specified time*

Computing Discounted Payback for the Project

- Assume we will accept the project if it pays back on a discounted basis in 2 years.
- Compute the PV for each cash flow and determine the payback period using discounted cash flows
    - Year 1: $165,000 - 63,120/1.12^1 = 108,643$
    - Year 2: $108,643 - 70,800/1.12^2 = 52,202$
    - Year 3: $52,202 - 91,080/1.12^3 = -12,627$ project pays back in year 3
- ***Do we accept or reject the project?***

Decision Criteria Test – Discounted Payback

- Does the discounted payback rule account for the time value of money?
- Does the discounted payback rule account for the risk of the cash flows?
- Does the discounted payback rule provide an indication about the increase in value?
- Should we consider the discounted payback rule for our primary decision criteria?

9.17 Advantages and Disadvantages of Discounted Payback

- Advantages
  - Includes time value of money
  - Easy to understand
  - Does not accept negative estimated NPV investments
  - Biased towards liquidity
- Disadvantages
  - May reject positive NPV investments
  - Requires an arbitrary cutoff point
  - Ignores cash flows beyond the cutoff point
  - Biased against long-term projects, such as R&D and new products

9.18 Average Accounting Return

- There are many different definitions for average accounting return
- The one used in the book is:
  - Average net income / average book value
  - Note that the average book value depends on how the asset is depreciated.
- Need to have a target cutoff rate
- Decision Rule: *Accept the project if the AAR is greater than a preset rate.*

Computing AAR For The Project

- Assume we require an average accounting return of 25%
- Average Net Income:
  - $(13{,}620 + 3{,}300 + 29{,}100) / 3 = 15{,}340$
- $AAR = 15{,}340 / 72{,}000 = .213 = 21.3\%$
- ***Do we accept or reject the project?***

Decision Criteria Test - AAR

- Does the AAR rule account for the time value of money?
- Does the AAR rule account for the risk of the cash flows?
- Does the AAR rule provide an indication about the increase in value?
- Should we consider the AAR rule for our primary decision criteria?

9.21 Advantages and Disadvantages of AAR

- Advantages
  - Easy to calculate
  - Needed information will usually be available
- Disadvantages
  - Not a true rate of return; time value of money is ignored
  - Uses an arbitrary benchmark cutoff rate
  - Based on accounting net income and book values, not cash flows and market values

9.22 Internal Rate of Return

- This is the most important alternative to NPV
- It is often used in practice and is intuitively appealing
- It is based entirely on the estimated cash flows and is independent of interest rates found elsewhere

9.23 IRR – Definition and Decision Rule

- Definition: IRR is the return that makes the NPV = 0
- Decision Rule: *Accept the project if the IRR is greater than the required return*

9.24 Computing IRR For The Project

- If you do not have a financial calculator, then this becomes a trial and error process
- Calculator
  - Enter the cash flows as you did with NPV
  - Press IRR and then CPT
  - IRR = 16.13% > 12% required return
- *Do we accept or reject the project?*

9.25 NPV Profile For The Project

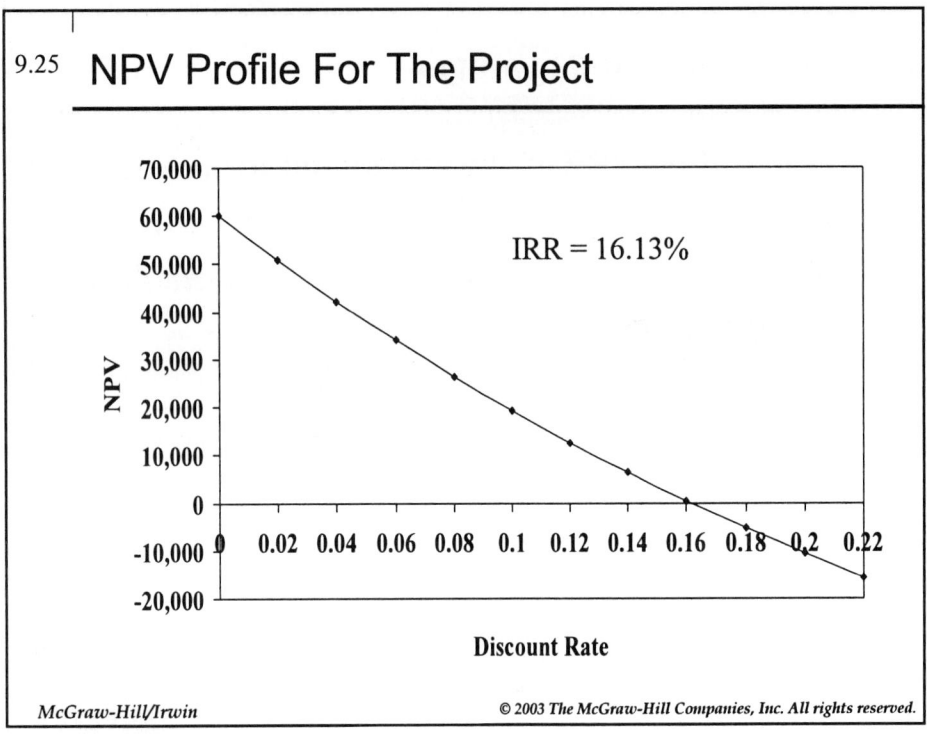

IRR = 16.13%

9.26 Decision Criteria Test - IRR

- Does the IRR rule account for the time value of money?
- Does the IRR rule account for the risk of the cash flows?
- Does the IRR rule provide an indication about the increase in value?
- Should we consider the IRR rule for our primary decision criteria?

9.27 Advantages of IRR

- Knowing a return is intuitively appealing
- It is a simple way to communicate the value of a project to someone who doesn't know all the estimation details
- If the IRR is high enough, you may not need to estimate a required return, which is often a difficult task

9.28 Summary of Decisions For The Project

Summary	
Net Present Value	*Accept*
Payback Period	*Reject*
Discounted Payback Period	*Reject*
Average Accounting Return	*Reject*
Internal Rate of Return	*Accept*

Calculating IRRs With A Spreadsheet

- You start with the cash flows the same as you did for the NPV
- You use the IRR function
  - You first enter your range of cash flows, beginning with the initial cash flow
  - You can enter a guess, but it is not necessary
  - The default format is a whole percent – you will normally want to increase the decimal places to at least two

NPV Vs. IRR

- NPV and IRR will generally give us the same decision
- Exceptions
  - Non-conventional cash flows – cash flow signs change more than once
  - Mutually exclusive projects
    - Initial investments are substantially different
    - Timing of cash flows is substantially different

IRR and Non-conventional Cash Flows

- When the cash flows change sign more than once, there is more than one IRR
- When you solve for IRR you are solving for the root of an equation and when you cross the x-axis more than once, there will be more than one return that solves the equation
- If you have more than one IRR, which one do you use to make your decision?

Another Example – Non-conventional Cash Flows

- Suppose an investment will cost $90,000 initially and will generate the following cash flows:
    - Year 1: 132,000
    - Year 2: 100,000
    - Year 3: -150,000
- The required return is 15%.
- Should we accept or reject the project?

9.33 NPV Profile

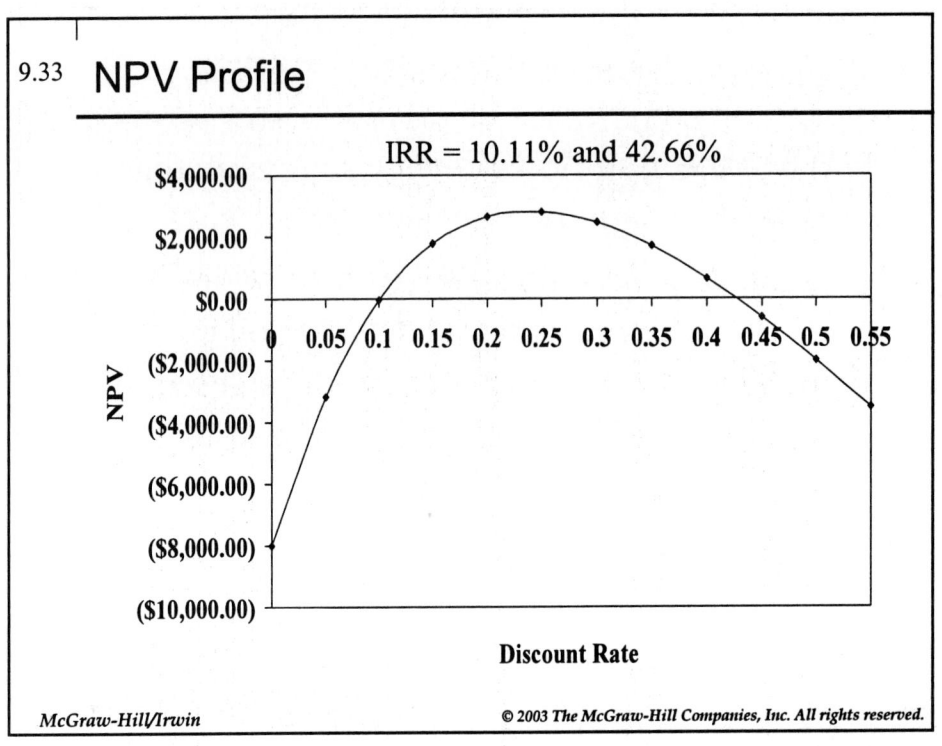

9.34 Summary of Decision Rules

- The NPV is positive at a required return of 15%, so you should *Accept*
- If you use the financial calculator, you would get an IRR of 10.11% which would tell you to *Reject*
- You need to recognize that there are non-conventional cash flows and look at the NPV profile

9.35 IRR and Mutually Exclusive Projects

- Mutually exclusive projects
  - If you choose one, you can't choose the other
  - Example: You can choose to attend graduate school next year at either Harvard or Stanford, but not both
- Intuitively you would use the following decision rules:
  - NPV – choose the project with the higher NPV
  - IRR – choose the project with the higher IRR

9.36 Example With Mutually Exclusive Projects

Period	Project A	Project B
0	-500	-400
1	325	325
2	325	200
IRR	19.43%	22.17%
NPV	64.05	60.74

The required return for both projects is 10%.

Which project should you accept and why?

9.37 NPV Profiles

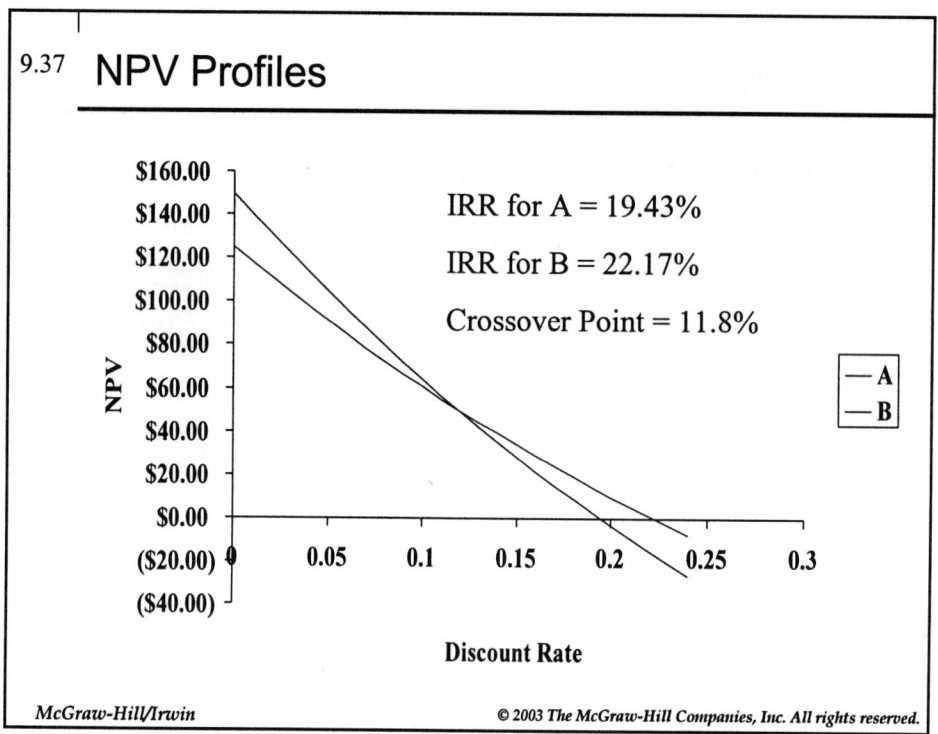

IRR for A = 19.43%

IRR for B = 22.17%

Crossover Point = 11.8%

9.38 Conflicts Between NPV and IRR

- NPV directly measures the increase in value to the firm
- Whenever there is a conflict between NPV and another decision rule, you should *always* use NPV
- IRR is unreliable in the following situations
  - Non-conventional cash flows
  - Mutually exclusive projects

9.39 Profitability Index

- Measures the benefit per unit cost, based on the time value of money
- A profitability index of 1.1 implies that for every $1 of investment, we create an additional $0.10 in value
- This measure can be very useful in situations where we have limited capital

9.40 Advantages and Disadvantages of Profitability Index

- Advantages
  - Closely related to NPV, generally leading to identical decisions
  - Easy to understand and communicate
  - May be useful when available investment funds are limited
- Disadvantages
  - May lead to incorrect decisions in comparisons of mutually exclusive investments

Capital Budgeting In Practice

- We should consider several investment criteria when making decisions
- NPV and IRR are the most commonly used primary investment criteria
- Payback is a commonly used secondary investment criteria

Summary – Discounted Cash Flow Criteria

- Net present value
  - Difference between market value and cost
  - Take the project if the NPV is positive
  - Has no serious problems
  - Preferred decision criterion
- Internal rate of return
  - Discount rate that makes NPV = 0
  - Take the project if the IRR is greater than required return
  - Same decision as NPV with conventional cash flows
  - IRR is unreliable with non-conventional cash flows or mutually exclusive projects
- Profitability Index
  - Benefit-cost ratio
  - Take investment if PI > 1
  - Cannot be used to rank mutually exclusive projects
  - May be use to rank projects in the presence of capital rationing

Summary – Payback Criteria

- Payback period
  - Length of time until initial investment is recovered
  - Take the project if it pays back in some specified period
  - Doesn't account for time value of money and there is an arbitrary cutoff period
- Discounted payback period
  - Length of time until initial investment is recovered on a discounted basis
  - Take the project if it pays back in some specified period
  - There is an arbitrary cutoff period

Summary – Accounting Criterion

- Average Accounting Return
  - Measure of accounting profit relative to book value
  - Similar to return on assets measure
  - Take the investment if the AAR exceeds some specified return level
  - Serious problems and should not be used

Quick Quiz

- Consider an investment that costs $100,000 and has a cash inflow of $25,000 every year for 5 years. The required return is 9% and required payback is 4 years.
    - What is the payback period?
    - What is the discounted payback period?
    - What is the NPV?
    - What is the IRR?
    - Should we accept the project?
- What decision rule should be the primary decision method?
- When is the IRR rule unreliable?

10.1 Key Concepts and Skills

- Understand how to determine the relevant cash flows for various types of proposed investments
- Be able to compute depreciation expense for tax purposes
- Understand the various methods for computing operating cash flow

10.2 Chapter Outline

- Project Cash Flows: A First Look
- Incremental Cash Flows
- Pro Forma Financial Statements and Project Cash Flows
- More on Project Cash Flow
- Alternative Definitions of Operating Cash Flow
- Some Special Cases of Cash Flow Analysis

10.3 Relevant Cash Flows

- The cash flows that should be included in a capital budgeting analysis are those that will only occur if the project is accepted
- These cash flows are called *incremental cash flows*
- The *stand-alone principle* allows us to analyze each project in isolation from the firm simply by focusing on incremental cash flows

10.4 Asking the Right Question

- You should always ask yourself "Will this cash flow occur ONLY if we accept the project?"
  - If the answer is "yes", it should be included in the analysis because it is incremental
  - If the answer is "no", it should not be included in the analysis because it will occur anyway
  - If the answer is "part of it", then we should include the part that occurs because of the project

10.5 Common Types of Cash Flows

- Sunk costs – costs that have accrued in the past
- Opportunity costs – costs of lost options
- Side effects
  - Positive side effects – benefits to other projects
  - Negative side effects – costs to other projects
- Changes in net working capital
- Financing costs
- Taxes

10.6 Pro Forma Statements and Cash Flow

- Capital budgeting relies heavily on pro forma accounting statements, particularly income statements
- Computing cash flows – refresher
  - Operating Cash Flow (OCF) = EBIT + depreciation – taxes
  - OCF = Net income + depreciation when there is no interest expense
  - Cash Flow From Assets (CFFA) = OCF – net capital spending (NCS) – changes in NWC

Table 10.1 Pro Forma Income Statement

Sales (50,000 units at $4.00/unit)	$200,000
Variable Costs ($2.50/unit)	125,000
Gross profit	$ 75,000
Fixed costs	12,000
Depreciation ($90,000 / 3)	30,000
EBIT	$ 33,000
Taxes (34%)	11,220
Net Income	$ 21,780

Table 10.2 Projected Capital Requirements

	Year			
	0	1	2	3
NWC	$20,000	$20,000	$20,000	$20,000
Net Fixed Assets	90,000	60,000	30,000	0
Total Investment	$110,000	$80,000	$50,000	$20,000

Table 10.5 Projected Total Cash Flows

	Year			
	0	1	2	3
OCF		$51,780	$51,780	$51,780
Change in NWC	-$20,000			20,000
Capital Spending	-$90,000			
CFFA	-$110,00	$51,780	$51,780	$71,780

Making The Decision

- Now that we have the cash flows, we can apply the techniques that we learned in chapter 9
- Enter the cash flows into the calculator and compute NPV and IRR
    - CF_0 = -110,000; C01 = 51,780; F01 = 2; C02 = 71,780
    - NPV; I = 20; CPT NPV = 10,648
    - CPT IRR = 25.8%
- *Should we accept or reject the project?*

10.11 More on NWC

- Why do we have to consider changes in NWC separately?
  - GAAP requires that sales be recorded on the income statement when made, not when cash is received
  - GAAP also requires that we record cost of goods sold when the corresponding sales are made, regardless of whether we have actually paid our suppliers yet
  - Finally, we have to buy inventory to support sales although we haven't collected cash yet

10.12 Depreciation

- The depreciation expense used for capital budgeting should be the depreciation schedule required by the IRS for tax purposes
- Depreciation itself is a non-cash expense, consequently, it is only relevant because it affects taxes
- Depreciation tax shield = DT
  - D = depreciation expense
  - T = marginal tax rate

10.13 Computing Depreciation

- Straight-line depreciation
  - D = (Initial cost − salvage) / number of years
  - Very few assets are depreciated straight-line for tax purposes
- MACRS
  - Need to know which asset class is appropriate for tax purposes
  - Multiply percentage given in table by the initial cost
  - Depreciate to zero
  - Mid-year convention

10.14 After-tax Salvage

- If the salvage value is different from the book value of the asset, then there is a tax effect
- Book value = initial cost − accumulated depreciation
- After-tax salvage = salvage − T(salvage − book value)

Example: Depreciation and After-tax Salvage

- You purchase equipment for $100,000 and it costs $10,000 to have it delivered and installed. Based on past information, you believe that you can sell the equipment for $17,000 when you are done with it in 6 years. The company's marginal tax rate is 40%. What is the depreciation expense each year and the after-tax salvage in year 6 for each of the following situations?

Example: Straight-line Depreciation

- Suppose the appropriate depreciation schedule is straight-line
    - D = (110,000 – 17,000) / 6 = 15,500 every year for 6 years
    - BV in year 6 = 110,000 – 6(15,500) = 17,000
    - After-tax salvage = 17,000 - .4(17,000 – 17,000) = 17,000

10.17 Example: Three-year MACRS

Year	MACRS percent	D
1	.3333	.3333(110,000) = 36,663
2	.4444	.4444(110,000) = 48,884
3	.1482	.1482(110,000) = 16,302
4	.0741	.0741(110,000) = 8,151

BV in year 6 = 110,000 − 36,663 − 48,884 − 16,302 − 8,151 = 0

After-tax salvage = 17,000 − .4(17,000 − 0) = $10,200

10.18 Example: 7-Year MACRS

Year	MACRS Percent	D
1	.1429	.1429(110,000) = 15,719
2	.2449	.2449(110,000) = 26,939
3	.1749	.1749(110,000) = 19,239
4	.1249	.1249(110,000) = 13,739
5	.0893	.0893(110,000) = 9,823
6	.0893	.0893(110,000) = 9,823

BV in year 6 = 110,000 − 15,719 − 26,939 − 19,239 − 13,739 − 9,823 − 9,823 = 14,718

After-tax salvage = 17,000 − .4(17,000 − 14,718) = 16,087.20

10.19 Example: Replacement Problem

- Original Machine
  - Initial cost = 100,000
  - Annual depreciation = 9000
  - Purchased 5 years ago
  - Book Value = 55,000
  - Salvage today = 65,000
  - Salvage in 5 years = 10,000

- New Machine
  - Initial cost = 150,000
  - 5-year life
  - Salvage in 5 years = 0
  - Cost savings = 50,000 per year
  - 3-year MACRS depreciation
- Required return = 10%
- Tax rate = 40%

10.20 Replacement Problem – Computing Cash Flows

- Remember that we are interested in incremental cash flows
- If we buy the new machine, then we will sell the old machine
- What are the cash flow consequences of selling the old machine today instead of in 5 years?

10.21 Replacement Problem – Pro Forma Income Statements

Year	1	2	3	4	5
Cost Savings	50,000	50,000	50,000	50,000	50,000
Depr.					
New	49,500	67,500	22,500	10,500	0
Old	9,000	9,000	9,000	9,000	9,000
Increm.	40,500	58,500	13,500	1,500	(9,000)
EBIT	9,500	(8,500)	36,500	48,500	59,000
Taxes	3,800	(3,400)	14,600	19,400	23,600
NI	5,700	(5,100)	21,900	29,100	35,400

10.22 Replacement Problem – Incremental Net Capital Spending

- Year 0
  - Cost of new machine = 150,000 (outflow)
  - After-tax salvage on old machine = 65,000 - .4(65,000 – 55,000) = 61,000 (inflow)
  - Incremental net capital spending = 150,000 – 61,000 = 89,000 (outflow)
- Year 5
  - After-tax salvage on old machine = 10,000 - .4(10,000 – 10,000) = 10,000 (outflow because we no longer receive this)

10.23 Replacement Problem – Cash Flow From Assets

Year	0	1	2	3	4	5
OCF		46,200	53,400	35,400	30,600	26,400
NCS	-89,000					-10,000
Δ In NWC	0					0
CFFA	-89,000	46,200	53,400	35,400	30,600	16,400

10.24 Replacement Problem – Analyzing the Cash Flows

- Now that we have the cash flows, we can compute the NPV and IRR
  - Enter the cash flows
  - Compute NPV = 54,812.10
  - Compute IRR = 36.28%
- *Should the company replace the equipment?*

Other Methods for Computing OCF

- Bottom-Up Approach
  - Works only when there is no interest expense
  - OCF = NI + depreciation
- Top-Down Approach
  - OCF = Sales – Costs – Taxes
  - Don't subtract non-cash deductions
- Tax Shield Approach
  - OCF = (Sales – Costs)(1 – T) + Depreciation*T

Example: Cost Cutting

- Your company is considering new computer system that will initially cost $1 million. It will save $300,000 a year in inventory and receivables management costs. The system is expected to last for five years and will be depreciated using 3-year MACRS. The system is expected to have a salvage value of $50,000 at the end of year 5. There is no impact on net working capital. The marginal tax rate is 40%. The required return is 8%.
- Click on the Excel icon to work through the example

10.27 Example: Setting the Bid Price

- Consider the example in the book:
  - Need to produce 5 modified trucks per year for 4 years
  - We can buy the truck platforms for $10,000 each
  - Facilities will be leased for $24,000 per year
  - Labor and material costs are $4,000 per truck
  - Need $60,000 investment in new equipment, depreciated straight-line to a zero salvage
  - Actually expect to sell it for $5000 at the end of 4 years
  - Need $40,000 in net working capital
  - Tax rate is 39%
  - Required return is 20%

10.28 Example: Equivalent Annual Cost Analysis

- Machine A
  - Initial Cost = $5,000,000
  - Pre-tax operating cost = $500,000
  - Straight-line depreciation over 5 year life
  - Expected salvage = $400,000

- Machine B
  - Initial Cost = $6,000,000
  - Pre-tax operating cost = $450,000
  - Straight-line depreciation over 8 year life
  - Expected salvage = $700,000

The machine chosen will be replaced indefinitely and neither machine will have a differential impact on revenue. No change in NWC is required.

The required return is 9% and the tax rate is 40%.

Quick Quiz

- How do we determine if cash flows are relevant to the capital budgeting decision?
- What are the different methods for computing operating cash flow and when are they important?
- What is the basic process for finding the bid price?
- What is equivalent annual cost and when should it be used?

11.1 Key Concepts and Skills

- Understand forecasting risk and sources of value
- Understand and be able to do scenario and sensitivity analysis
- Understand the various forms of break-even analysis
- Understand operating leverage
- Understand capital rationing

11.2 Chapter Outline

- Evaluating NPV Estimates
- Scenario and Other What-If Analyses
- Break-Even Analysis
- Operating Cash Flow, Sales Volume, and Break-Even
- Operating Leverage
- Capital Rationing

11.3 Evaluating NPV Estimates

- The NPV estimates are just that – estimates
- A positive NPV is a good start – now we need to take a closer look
  - Forecasting risk – how sensitive is our NPV to changes in the cash flow estimates, the more sensitive, the greater the forecasting risk
  - Sources of value – why does this project create value?

11.4 Scenario Analysis

- What happens to the NPV under different cash flows scenarios?
- At the very least look at:
  - Best case – revenues are high and costs are low
  - Worst case – revenues are low and costs are high
  - Measure of the range of possible outcomes
- Best case and worst case are not necessarily probable, they can still be possible

11.5 New Project Example

- Consider the project discussed in the text
- The initial cost is $200,000 and the project has a 5-year life. There is no salvage. Depreciation is straight-line, the required return is 12% and the tax rate is 34%
- The base case NPV is 15,567

11.6 Summary of Scenario Analysis

Scenario	Net Income	Cash Flow	NPV	IRR
Base case	19,800	59,800	15,567	15.1%
Worst Case	-15,510	24,490	-111,719	-14.4%
Best Case	59,730	99,730	159,504	40.9%

11.7 Sensitivity Analysis

- What happens to NPV when we vary one variable at a time
- This is a subset of scenario analysis where we are looking at the effect of specific variables on NPV
- The greater the volatility in NPV in relation to a specific variable, the larger the forecasting risk associated with that variable and the more attention we want to pay to its estimation

11.8 Summary of Sensitivity Analysis for New Project

Scenario	Unit Sales	Cash Flow	NPV	IRR
Base case	6000	59,800	15,567	15.1%
Worst case	5500	53,200	-8,226	10.3%
Best case	6500	66,400	39,357	19.7%

11.9 Simulation Analysis

- Simulation is really just an expanded sensitivity and scenario analysis
- Monte Carlo simulation can estimate thousands of possible outcomes based on conditional probability distributions and constraints for each of the variables
- The output is a probability distribution for NPV with an estimate of the probability of obtaining a positive net present value
- The simulation only works as well as the information that is entered and very bad decisions can be made if care is not taken to analyze the interaction between variables

11.10 Making A Decision

- Beware "Paralysis of Analysis"
- At some point you have to make a decision
- If the majority of your scenarios have positive NPVs, then you can feel reasonably comfortable about accepting the project
- If you have a crucial variable that leads to a negative NPV with a small change in the estimates, then you may want to forego the project

11.11 Break-Even Analysis

- Common tool for analyzing the relationship between sales volume and profitability
- There are three common break-even measures
  - Accounting break-even – sales volume where net income = 0
  - Cash break-even – sales volume where operating cash flow = 0
  - Financial break-even – sales volume where net present value = 0

11.12 Example: Costs

- There are two types of costs that are important in breakeven analysis: variable and fixed
  - Total variable costs = quantity * cost per unit
  - Fixed costs are constant, regardless of output, over some time period
  - Total costs = fixed + variable = FC + vQ
- Example:
  - Your firm pays $3000 per month in fixed costs. You also pay $15 per unit to produce your product.
    - What is your total cost if you produce 1000 units?
    - What if you produce 5000 units?

11.13 Average vs. Marginal Cost

- Average Cost
  - TC / # of units
  - Will decrease as # of units increases
- Marginal Cost
  - The cost to produce one more unit
  - Same as variable cost per unit
- Example: What is the average cost and marginal cost under each situation in the previous example
  - Produce 1000 units: Average = 18,000 / 1000 = $18
  - Produce 5000 units: Average = 78,000 / 5000 = $15.60

11.14 Accounting Break-Even

- The quantity that leads to a zero net income
- $NI = (Sales - VC - FC - D)(1 - T) = 0$
- $QP - vQ - FC - D = 0$
- $Q(P - v) = FC + D$
- $Q = (FC + D) / (P - v)$

Using Accounting Break-Even

- Accounting break-even is often used as an early stage screening number
- If a project cannot break-even on an accounting basis, then it is not going to be a worthwhile project
- Accounting break-even gives managers an indication of how a project will impact accounting profit

Accounting Break-Even and Cash Flow

- We are more interested in cash flow than we are in accounting numbers
- As long as a firm has non-cash deductions, there will be a positive cash flow
- If a firm just breaks-even on an accounting basis, cash flow = depreciation
- If a firm just breaks-even on an accounting basis, NPV < 0

Example

- Consider the following project
    - A new product requires an initial investment of $5 million and will be depreciated to an expected salvage of zero over 5 years
    - The price of the new product is expected to be $25,000 and the variable cost per unit is $15,000
    - The fixed cost is $1 million
    - What is the accounting break-even point each year?
        - Depreciation = 5,000,000 / 5 = 1,000,000
        - Q = (1,000,000 + 1,000,000)/(25,000 – 15,000) = 200 units

Sales Volume and Operating Cash Flow

- What is the operating cash flow at the accounting break-even point (ignoring taxes)?
    - OCF = (S – VC – FC - D) + D
    - OCF = (200*25,000 – 200*15,000 – 1,000,000) + 1,000,000 = 1,000,000
- What is the cash break-even quantity?
    - OCF = [(P-v)Q – FC – D] + D = (P-v)Q – FC
    - Q = (OCF + FC) / (P – v)
    - Q = (0 + 1,000,000) / (25,000 – 15,000) = 100 units

11.19 Three Types of Break-Even Analysis

- Accounting Break-even
  - Where NI = 0
  - $Q = (FC + D)/(P - v)$
- Cash Break-even
  - Where OCF = 0
  - $Q = (FC + OCF)/(P - v)$ (ignoring taxes)
- Financial Break-even
  - Where NPV = 0
- Cash BE < Accounting BE < Financial BE

11.20 Example: Break-Even Analysis

- Consider the previous example
  - Assume a required return of 18%
  - Accounting break-even = 200
  - Cash break-even = 100
  - What is the financial break-even point?
    - Similar process to finding the bid price
    - What OCF (or payment) makes NPV = 0?
      - N = 5; PV = 5,000,000; I/Y = 18; CPT PMT = 1,598,889 = OCF
    - Q = (1,000,000 + 1,598,889) / (25,000 − 15,000) = 260 units
- The question now becomes: Can we sell at least 260 units per year?

Operating Leverage

- Operating leverage is the relationship between sales and operating cash flow
- Degree of operating leverage measures this relationship
    - The higher the DOL, the greater the variability in operating cash flow
    - The higher the fixed costs, the higher the DOL
    - DOL depends on the sales level you are starting from
- DOL = 1 + (FC / OCF)

Example: DOL

- Consider the previous example
- Suppose sales are 300 units
    - This meets all three break-even measures
    - What is the DOL at this sales level?
    - OCF = (25,000 – 15,000)*300 – 1,000,000 = 2,000,000
    - DOL = 1 + 1,000,000 / 2,000,000 = 1.5
- What will happen to OCF if unit sales increases by 20%?
    - Percentage change in OCF = DOL*Percentage change in Q
    - Percentage change in OCF = 1.5(.2) = .3 or 30%
    - OCF would increase to 2,000,000(1.3) = 2,600,000

11.23 Capital Rationing

- Capital rationing occurs when a firm or division has limited resources
  - Soft rationing – the limited resources are temporary, often self-imposed
  - Hard rationing – capital will never be available for this project
- The profitability index is a useful tool when faced with soft rationing

11.24 Quick Quiz

- What is sensitivity analysis, scenario analysis and simulation?
- Why are these analyses important and how should they be used?
- What are the three types of break-even and how should each be used?
- What is degree of operating leverage?
- What is the difference between hard rationing and soft rationing?

12.1 Key Concepts and Skills

- Know how to calculate the return on an investment
- Understand the historical returns on various types of investments
- Understand the historical risks on various types of investments

12.2 Chapter Outline

- Returns
- The Historical Record
- Average Returns: The First Lesson
- The Variability of Returns: The Second Lesson
- Capital Market Efficiency

12.3 Risk, Return and Financial Markets

- We can examine returns in the financial markets to help us determine the appropriate returns on non-financial assets
- Lesson from capital market history
  - There is a reward for bearing risk
  - The greater the potential reward, the greater the risk
  - This is called the risk-return trade-off

12.4 Dollar Returns

- Total dollar return = income from investment + capital gain (loss) due to change in price
- Example:
  - You bought a bond for $950 1 year ago. You have received two coupons of $30 each. You can sell the bond for $975 today. What is your total dollar return?
    - Income = 30 + 30 = 60
    - Capital gain = 975 − 950 = 25
    - Total dollar return = 60 + 25 = $85

12.5 Percentage Returns

- It is generally more intuitive to think in terms of percentages than dollar returns
- Dividend yield = income / beginning price
- Capital gains yield = (ending price – beginning price) / beginning price
- Total percentage return = dividend yield + capital gains yield

12.6 Example – Calculating Returns

- You bought a stock for $35 and you received dividends of $1.25. The stock is now selling for $40.
    - What is your dollar return?
        - Dollar return = 1.25 + (40 – 35) = $6.25
    - What is your percentage return?
        - Dividend yield = 1.25 / 35 = 3.57%
        - Capital gains yield = (40 – 35) / 35 = 14.29%
        - Total percentage return = 3.57 + 14.29 = 17.86%

12.7 The Importance of Financial Markets

- Financial markets allow companies, governments and individuals to increase their utility
  - Savers have the ability to invest in financial assets so that they can defer consumption and earn a return to compensate them for doing so
  - Borrowers have better access to the capital that is available so that they can invest in productive assets
- Financial markets also provide us with information about the returns that are required for various levels of risk

12.8 Figure 12.4

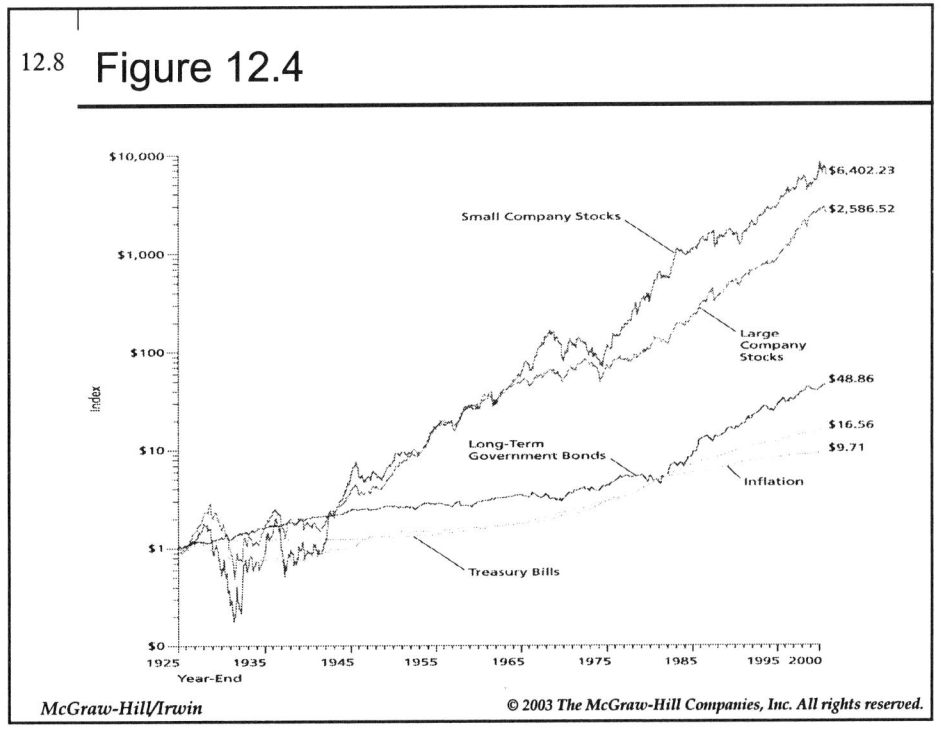

12.9 Year-to-Year Total Returns

Large-Company Stock Returns

Large Companies

Long-Term Government Bond Returns

Long-Term Government Bonds

U.S. Treasury Bill Returns

U.S. Treasury Bills

12.10 Average Returns

Investment	Average Return
Large stocks	13.0%
Small Stocks	17.3%
Long-term Corporate Bonds	6.0%
Long-term Government Bonds	5.7%
U.S. Treasury Bills	3.9%
Inflation	3.2%

12.11 Risk Premiums

- The "extra" return earned for taking on risk
- Treasury bills are considered to be risk-free
- The risk premium is the return over and above the risk-free rate

12.12 Historical Risk Premiums

- Large stocks: $13.0 - 3.9 = 9.1\%$
- Small stocks: $17.3 - 3.9 = 13.4\%$
- Long-term corporate bonds: $6.0 - 3.9 = 2.1\%$
- Long-term government bonds: $5.7 - 3.9 = 1.8\%$

Figure 12.9

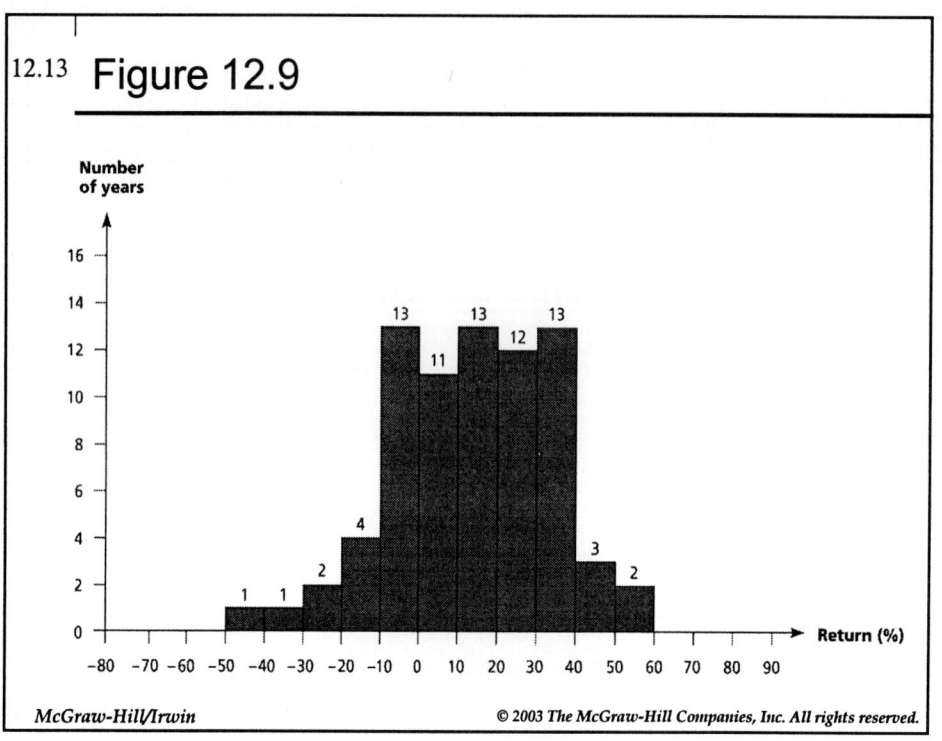

Variance and Standard Deviation

- Variance and standard deviation measure the volatility of asset returns
- The greater the volatility the greater the uncertainty
- Historical variance = sum of squared deviations from the mean / (number of observations − 1)
- Standard deviation = square root of the variance

12.15 Example – Variance and Standard Deviation

Year	Actual Return	Average Return	Deviation from the Mean	Squared Deviation
1	.15	.105	.045	.002025
2	.09	.105	-.015	.000225
3	.06	.105	-.045	.002025
4	.12	.105	.015	.000225
Totals	.42		.00	.0045

Variance = .0045 / (4-1) = .0015   Standard Deviation = .03873

12.16 Work the Web Example

- How volatile are mutual funds?
- Morningstar provides information on mutual funds, including volatility
- Click on the web surfer to go to the Morningstar site
  - Pick a fund, such as the Aim European Development fund (AEDCX)
  - Enter the ticker, press go and then scroll down to volatility

12.17
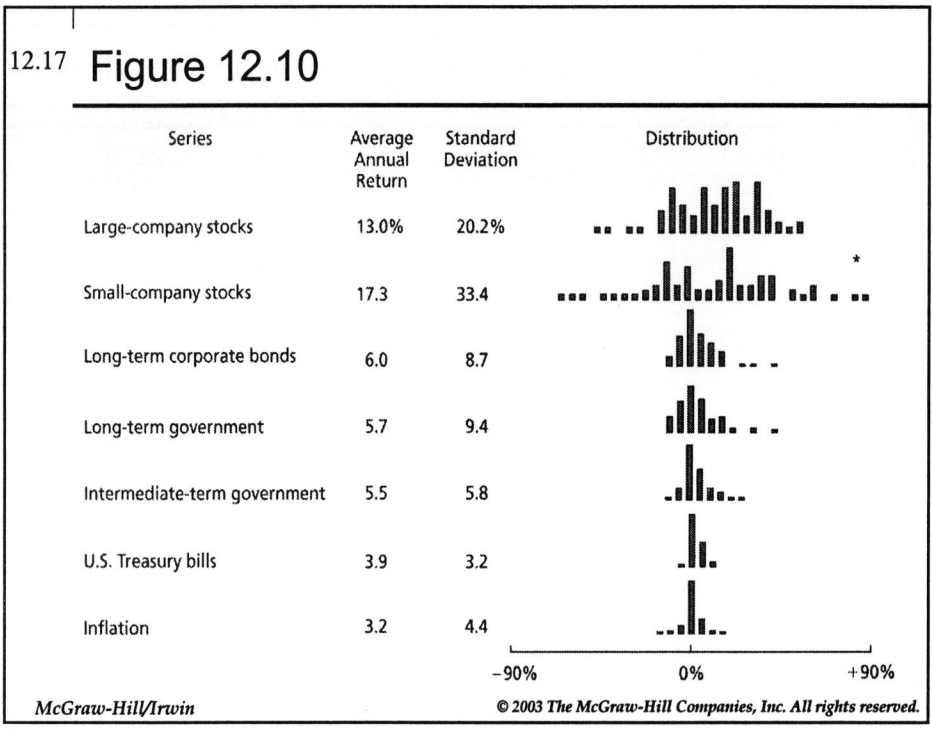
Figure 12.10

12.18
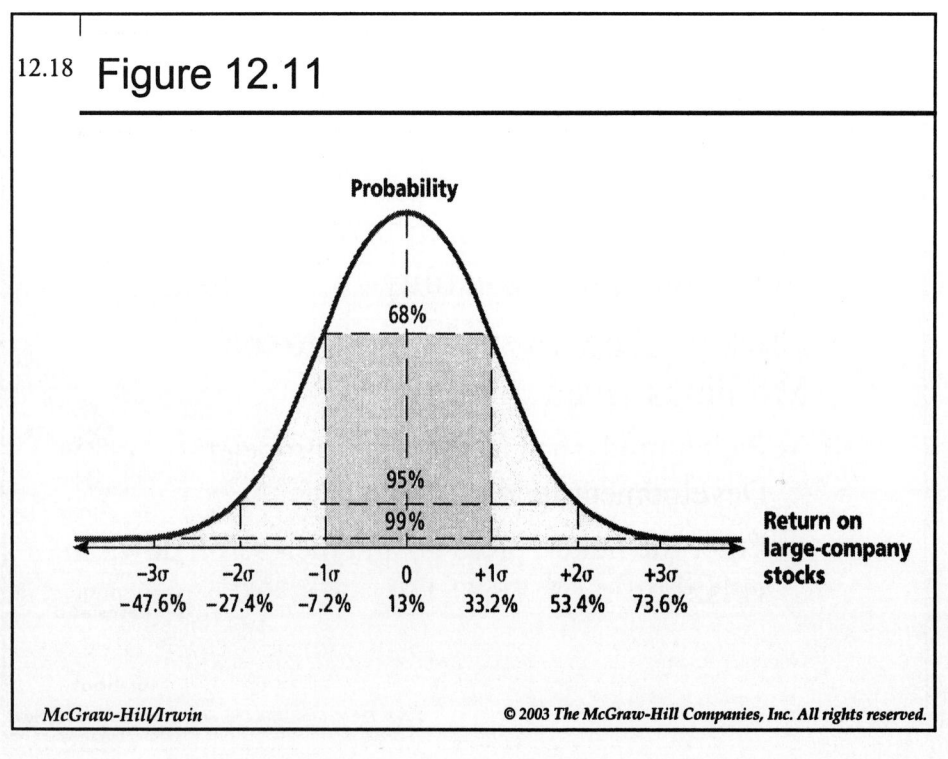
Figure 12.11

12.19 Efficient Capital Markets

- Stock prices are in equilibrium or are "fairly" priced
- If this is true, then you should not be able to earn "abnormal" or "excess" returns
- Efficient markets *DO NOT* imply that investors cannot earn a positive return in the stock market

12.20 Figure 12.12

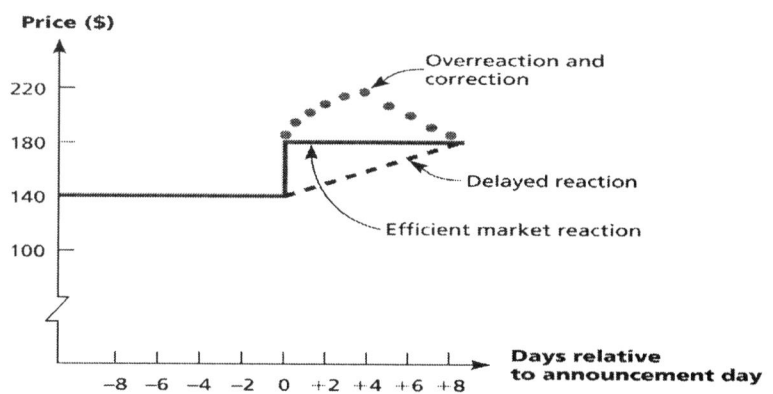

Efficient market reaction: The price instantaneously adjusts to and fully reflects new information; there is no tendency for subsequent increases and decreases to occur.
Delayed reaction: The price partially adjusts to the new information; 8 days elapse before the price completely reflects the new information.
Overreaction: The price overadjusts to the new information; it overshoots the new price and subsequently corrects.

What Makes Markets Efficient?

- There are many investors out there doing research
  - As new information comes to market, this information is analyzed and trades are made based on this information
  - Therefore, prices should reflect all available public information
- If investors stop researching stocks, then the market will not be efficient

Common Misconceptions about EMH

- Efficient markets do not mean that you can't make money
- They do mean that, on average, you will earn a return that is appropriate for the risk undertaken and there is not a bias in prices that can be exploited to earn excess returns
- Market efficiency will not protect you from wrong choices if you do not diversify – you still don't want to put all your eggs in one basket

Strong Form Efficiency

- Prices reflect all information, including public and private
- If the market is strong form efficient, then investors could not earn abnormal returns regardless of the information they possessed
- Empirical evidence indicates that markets are NOT strong form efficient and that insiders could earn abnormal returns

Semistrong Form Efficiency

- Prices reflect all publicly available information including trading information, annual reports, press releases, etc.
- If the market is semistrong form efficient, then investors cannot earn abnormal returns by trading on public information
- Implies that fundamental analysis will not lead to abnormal returns

12.25 Weak Form Efficiency

- Prices reflect all past market information such as price and volume
- If the market is weak form efficient, then investors cannot earn abnormal returns by trading on market information
- Implies that technical analysis will not lead to abnormal returns
- Empirical evidence indicates that markets are generally weak form efficient

12.26 Quick Quiz

- Which of the investments discussed have had the highest average return and risk premium?
- Which of the investments discussed have had the highest standard deviation?
- What is capital market efficiency?
- What are the three forms of market efficiency?

13.1 Key Concepts and Skills

- Know how to calculate expected returns
- Understand the impact of diversification
- Understand the systematic risk principle
- Understand the security market line
- Understand the risk-return trade-off
- Be able to use the Capital Asset Pricing Model

13.2 Chapter Outline

- Expected Returns and Variances
- Portfolios
- Announcements, Surprises, and Expected Returns
- Risk: Systematic and Unsystematic
- Diversification and Portfolio Risk
- Systematic Risk and Beta
- The Security Market Line
- The SML and the Cost of Capital: A Preview

13.3 Expected Returns

- Expected returns are based on the probabilities of possible outcomes
- In this context, "expected" means average if the process is repeated many times
- The "expected" return does not even have to be a possible return

$$E(R) = \sum_{i=1}^{n} p_i R_i$$

13.4 Example: Expected Returns

- Suppose you have predicted the following returns for stocks C and T in three possible states of nature. What are the expected returns?

State	Probability	C	T
Boom	0.3	0.15	0.25
Normal	0.5	0.10	0.20
Recession	???	0.02	0.01

- $R_C = .3(.15) + .5(.10) + .2(.02) = .099 = 9.99\%$
- $R_T = .3(.25) + .5(.20) + .2(.01) = .177 = 17.7\%$

13.5 Variance and Standard Deviation

- Variance and standard deviation still measure the volatility of returns
- Using unequal probabilities for the entire range of possibilities
- Weighted average of squared deviations

$$\sigma^2 = \sum_{i=1}^{n} p_i (R_i - E(R))^2$$

13.6 Example: Variance and Standard Deviation

- Consider the previous example. What are the variance and standard deviation for each stock?
- Stock C
  - $\sigma^2 = .3(.15-.099)^2 + .5(.1-.099)^2 + .2(.02-.099)^2 = .002029$
  - $\sigma = .045$
- Stock T
  - $\sigma^2 = .3(.25-.177)^2 + .5(.2-.177)^2 + .2(.01-.177)^2 = .007441$
  - $\sigma = .0863$

13.7 Another Example

- Consider the following information:
  - State   Probability   ABC, Inc.
  - Boom   .25   .15
  - Normal   .50   .08
  - Slowdown   .15   .04
  - Recession   .10   -.03
- What is the expected return?
- What is the variance?
- What is the standard deviation?

13.8 Portfolios

- A portfolio is a collection of assets
- An asset's risk and return is important in how it affects the risk and return of the portfolio
- The risk-return trade-off for a portfolio is measured by the portfolio expected return and standard deviation, just as with individual assets

13.9 Example: Portfolio Weights

- Suppose you have $15,000 to invest and you have purchased securities in the following amounts. What are your portfolio weights in each security?

    - $2000 of DCLK
    - $3000 of KO
    - $4000 of INTC
    - $6000 of KEI

- DCLK: 2/15 = .133
- KO: 3/15 = .2
- INTC: 4/15 = .267
- KEI: 6/15 = .4

13.10 Portfolio Expected Returns

- The expected return of a portfolio is the weighted average of the expected returns for each asset in the portfolio

$$E(R_P) = \sum_{j=1}^{m} w_j E(R_j)$$

- You can also find the expected return by finding the portfolio return in each possible state and computing the expected value as we did with individual securities

13.11 Example: Expected Portfolio Returns

- Consider the portfolio weights computed previously. If the individual stocks have the following expected returns, what is the expected return for the portfolio?
    - DCLK: 19.65%
    - KO: 8.96%
    - INTC: 9.67%
    - KEI: 8.13%
- $E(R_P) = .133(19.65) + .2(8.96) + .167(9.67) + .4(8.13) = 9.27\%$

13.12 Portfolio Variance

- Compute the portfolio return for each state:
$R_P = w_1R_1 + w_2R_2 + \ldots + w_mR_m$
- Compute the expected portfolio return using the same formula as for an individual asset
- Compute the portfolio variance and standard deviation using the same formulas as for an individual asset

13.13 Example: Portfolio Variance

- Consider the following information
  - Invest 50% of your money in Asset A
  - State   Probability   A   B   Portfolio
  - Boom   .4   30%   -5%   12.5%
  - Bust   .6   -10%   25%   7.5%
- What is the expected return and standard deviation for each asset?
- What is the expected return and standard deviation for the portfolio?

13.14 Another Example

- Consider the following information
  - State   Probability   X   Z
  - Boom   .25   15%   10%
  - Normal   .60   10%   9%
  - Recession   .15   5%   10%
- What is the expected return and standard deviation for a portfolio with an investment of $6000 in asset X and $4000 in asset Y?

13.15 Expected versus Unexpected Returns

- Realized returns are generally not equal to expected returns
- There is the expected component and the unexpected component
  - At any point in time, the unexpected return can be either positive or negative
  - Over time, the average of the unexpected component is zero

13.16 Announcements and News

- Announcements and news contain both an expected component and a surprise component
- It is the surprise component that affects a stock's price and therefore its return
- This is very obvious when we watch how stock prices move when an unexpected announcement is made or earnings are different than anticipated

13.17 Efficient Markets

- Efficient markets are a result of investors trading on the unexpected portion of announcements
- The easier it is to trade on surprises, the more efficient markets should be
- Efficient markets involve random price changes because we cannot predict surprises

13.18 Systematic Risk

- Risk factors that affect a large number of assets
- Also known as non-diversifiable risk or market risk
- Includes such things as changes in GDP, inflation, interest rates, etc.

13.19 Unsystematic Risk

- Risk factors that affect a limited number of assets
- Also known as unique risk and asset-specific risk
- Includes such things as labor strikes, part shortages, etc.

13.20 Returns

- Total Return = expected return + unexpected return
- Unexpected return = systematic portion + unsystematic portion
- Therefore, total return can be expressed as follows:
- Total Return = expected return + systematic portion + unsystematic portion

13.21 Diversification

- Portfolio diversification is the investment in several different asset classes or sectors
- Diversification is not just holding a lot of assets
- For example, if you own 50 internet stocks, you are not diversified
- However, if you own 50 stocks that span 20 different industries, then you are diversified

13.22 Table 13.7

(1) Number of Stocks in Portfolio	(2) Average Standard Deviation of Annual Portfolio Returns	(3) Ratio of Portfolio Standard Deviation to Standard Deviation of a Single Stock
1	49.24%	1.00
2	37.36	.76
4	29.69	.60
6	26.64	.54
8	24.98	.51
10	23.93	.49
20	21.68	.44
30	20.87	.42
40	20.46	.42
50	20.20	.41
100	19.69	.40
200	19.42	.39
300	19.34	.39
400	19.29	.39
500	19.27	.39
1,000	19.21	.39

These figures are from Table 1 in M. Statman, "How Many Stocks Make a Diversified Portfolio?" *Journal of Financial and Quantitative Analysis* 22 (September 1987), pp. 353–64. They were derived from E. J. Elton and M. J. Gruber, "Risk Reduction and Portfolio Size: An Analytic Solution," *Journal of Business* 50 (October 1977), pp. 415–37.

The Principle of Diversification

- Diversification can substantially reduce the variability of returns without an equivalent reduction in expected returns
- This reduction in risk arises because worse than expected returns from one asset are offset by better than expected returns from another
- However, there is a minimum level of risk that cannot be diversified away and that is the systematic portion

Figure 13.1

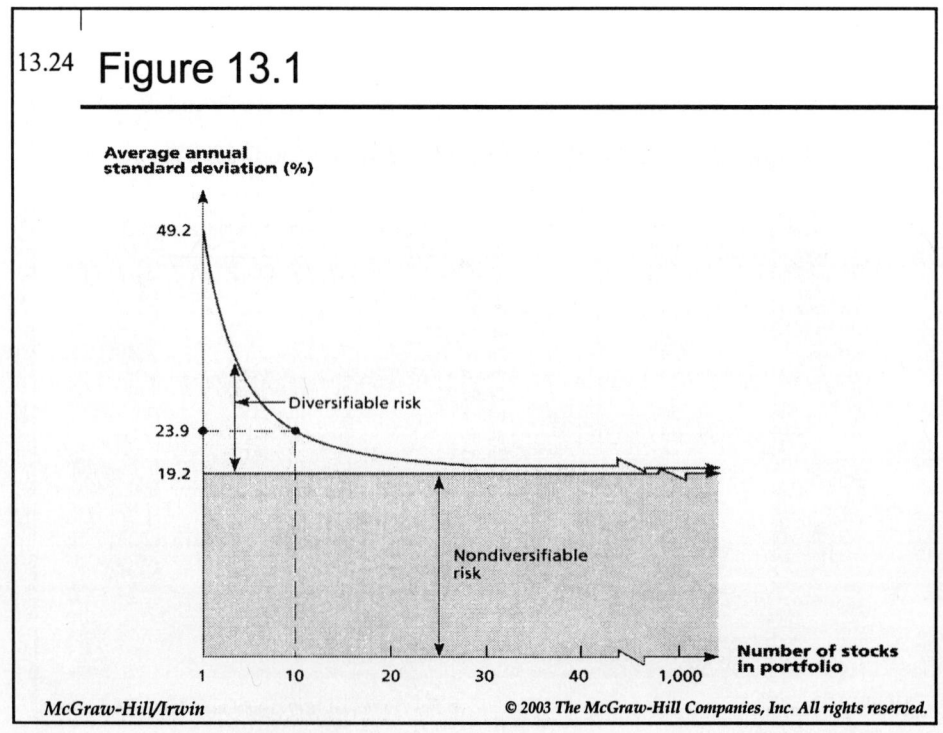

Diversifiable Risk

- The risk that can be eliminated by combining assets into a portfolio
- Often considered the same as unsystematic, unique or asset-specific risk
- If we hold only one asset, or assets in the same industry, then we are exposing ourselves to risk that we could diversify away

Total Risk

- Total risk = systematic risk + unsystematic risk
- The standard deviation of returns is a measure of total risk
- For well diversified portfolios, unsystematic risk is very small
- Consequently, the total risk for a diversified portfolio is essentially equivalent to the systematic risk

13.27 Systematic Risk Principle

- There is a reward for bearing risk
- There is not a reward for bearing risk unnecessarily
- The expected return on a risky asset depends only on that asset's systematic risk since unsystematic risk can be diversified away

13.28 Measuring Systematic Risk

- How do we measure systematic risk?
- We use the beta coefficient to measure systematic risk
- What does beta tell us?
  - A beta of 1 implies the asset has the same systematic risk as the overall market
  - A beta < 1 implies the asset has less systematic risk than the overall market
  - A beta > 1 implies the asset has more systematic risk than the overall market

Table 13.8

	Beta Coefficient (β_i)
American Electric Power	.55
Exxon	.75
IBM	.95
General Motors	1.05
Harley-Davidson	1.20
Abercrombie & Fitch	1.30
AOL-Time Warner	1.75

Source: *Value Line Investment Survey*, 2001.

Total versus Systematic Risk

- Consider the following information:

	Standard Deviation	Beta
– Security C	20%	1.25
– Security K	30%	0.95

- Which security has more total risk?
- Which security has more systematic risk?
- Which security should have the higher expected return?

13.31 Work the Web Example

- Many sites provide betas for companies
- Yahoo Finance provides beta, plus a lot of other information under its profile link
- Click on the web surfer to go to Yahoo Finance
  - Enter a ticker symbol and get a basic quote
  - Click on profile

13.32 Example: Portfolio Betas

- Consider the previous example with the following four securities

Security	Weight	Beta
DCLK	.133	3.69
KO	.2	0.64
INTC	.167	1.64
KEI	.4	1.79

- What is the portfolio beta?
- .133(3.69) + .2(.64) + .167(1.64) + .4(1.79) = 1.61

13.33 Beta and the Risk Premium

- Remember that the risk premium = expected return – risk-free rate
- The higher the beta, the greater the risk premium should be
- Can we define the relationship between the risk premium and beta so that we can estimate the expected return?
  - YES!

13.34 Example: Portfolio Expected Returns and Betas

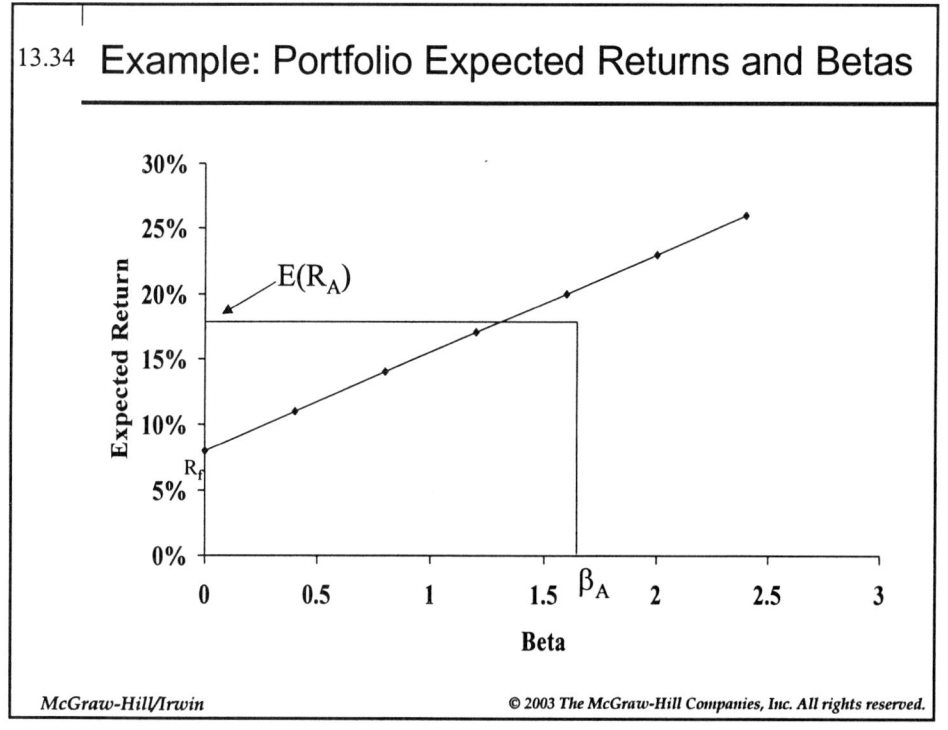

Reward-to-Risk Ratio: Definition and Example

- The reward-to-risk ratio is the slope of the line illustrated in the previous example
  - Slope = $(E(R_A) - R_f) / (\beta_A - 0)$
  - Reward-to-risk ratio for previous example = $(20 - 8) / (1.6 - 0) = 7.5$
- What if an asset has a reward-to-risk ratio of 8 (implying that the asset plots above the line)?
- What if an asset has a reward-to-risk ratio of 7 (implying that the asset plots below the line)?

Market Equilibrium

- In equilibrium, all assets and portfolios must have the same reward-to-risk ratio and they all must equal the reward-to-risk ratio for the market

$$\frac{E(R_A) - R_f}{\beta_A} = \frac{E(R_M - R_f)}{\beta_M}$$

13.37 Security Market Line

- The security market line (SML) is the representation of market equilibrium
- The slope of the SML is the reward-to-risk ratio: $(E(R_M) - R_f) / \beta_M$
- But since the beta for the market is ALWAYS equal to one, the slope can be rewritten
- Slope = $E(R_M) - R_f$ = market risk premium

13.38 The Capital Asset Pricing Model (CAPM)

- The capital asset pricing model defines the relationship between risk and return
- $E(R_A) = R_f + \beta_A(E(R_M) - R_f)$
- If we know an asset's systematic risk, we can use the CAPM to determine its expected return
- This is true whether we are talking about financial assets or physical assets

Factors Affecting Expected Return

- Pure time value of money – measured by the risk-free rate
- Reward for bearing systematic risk – measured by the market risk premium
- Amount of systematic risk – measured by beta

Example - CAPM

- Consider the betas for each of the assets given earlier. If the risk-free rate is 4.5% and the market risk premium is 8.5%, what is the expected return for each?

Security	Beta	Expected Return
DCLK	3.69	4.5 + 3.69(8.5) = 35.865%
KO	.64	4.5 + .64(8.5) = 9.940%
INTC	1.64	4.5 + 1.64(8.5) = 18.440%
KEI	1.79	4.5 + 1.79(8.5) = 19.715%

Figure 13.4

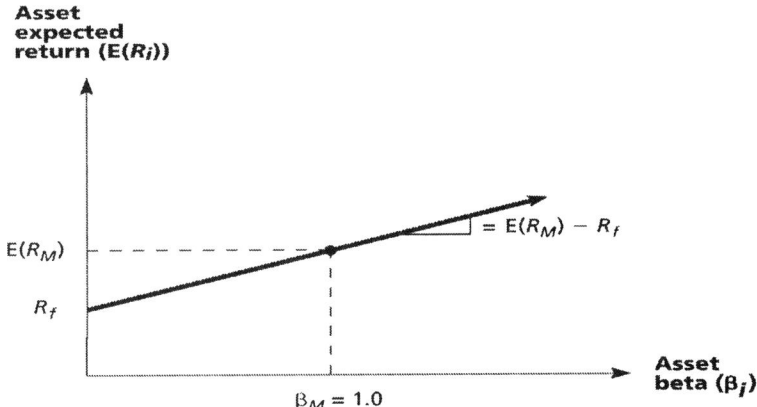

The slope of the security market line is equal to the market risk premium; i.e., the reward for bearing an average amount of systematic risk. The equation describing the SML can be written:

$$E(R_i) = R_f + \beta_i \times [E(R_M) - R_f]$$

which is the capital asset pricing model (CAPM).

Quick Quiz

- How do you compute the expected return and standard deviation for an individual asset? For a portfolio?
- What is the difference between systematic and unsystematic risk?
- What type of risk is relevant for determining the expected return?
- Consider an asset with a beta of 1.2, a risk-free rate of 5% and a market return of 13%.
  - What is the reward-to-risk ratio in equilibrium?
  - What is the expected return on the asset?

14.1 Key Concepts and Skills

- Understand the options terminology
- Be able to determine option payoffs and pricing bounds
- Understand the five major determinants of option value
- Understand employee stock options
- Understand the various managerial options
- Understand the differences between warrants and traditional call options
- Understand convertible securities and how to determine their value

14.2 Chapter Outline

- Options: The Basics
- Fundamentals of Option Valuation
- Valuing a Call Option
- Employee Stock Options
- Equity as a Call Option on the Firm's Assets
- Options and Capital Budgeting
- Options and Corporate Securities

14.3 Option Terminology

- Call
- Put
- Strike or Exercise price
- Expiration date
- Option premium
- Option writer
- American Option
- European Option

14.4 Stock Option Quotations

- Look at Table 14.1 in the book
  - Price and volume information for calls and puts with the same strike and expiration is provided on the same line
- Things to notice
  - Prices are higher for options with the same strike price but longer expirations
  - Call options with strikes less than the current price are worth more than the corresponding puts
  - Call options with strikes greater than the current price are worth less than the corresponding puts

14.5 Option Payoffs – Calls

- The value of the call at expiration is the intrinsic value
    - Max(0, S-E)
    - If S<E, then the payoff is 0
    - If S>E, then the payoff is S – E
- Assume that the exercise price is $35

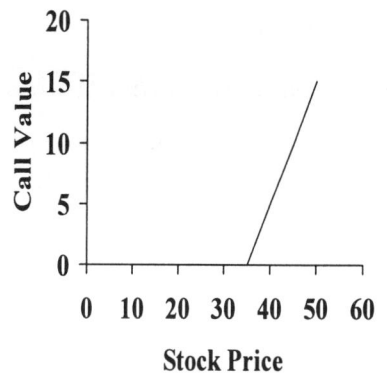

Call Option Payoff Diagram

14.6 Option Payoffs - Puts

- The value of a put at expiration is the intrinsic value
    - Max(0, E-S)
    - If S<E, then the payoff is E-S
    - If S>E, then the payoff is 0
- Assume that the exercise price is $35

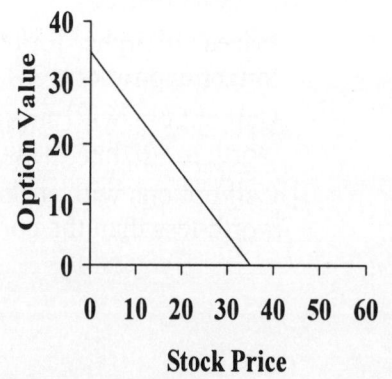

Payoff Diagram for Put Options

14.7 Work the Web Example

- Where can we find option prices?
- On the Internet, of course. One site that provides option prices is Yahoo Finance
- Click on the web surfer to go to Yahoo Finance
  - Enter a ticker symbol to get a basic quote
  - Follow the options link
  - Check out "symbology" to see how the ticker symbols are formed

14.8 Call Option Bounds

- Upper bound
  - Call price must be less than or equal to the stock price
- Lower bound
  - Call price must be greater than or equal to the stock price minus the exercise price or zero, whichever is greater
- If either of these bounds are violated, there is an arbitrage opportunity

Figure 14.2

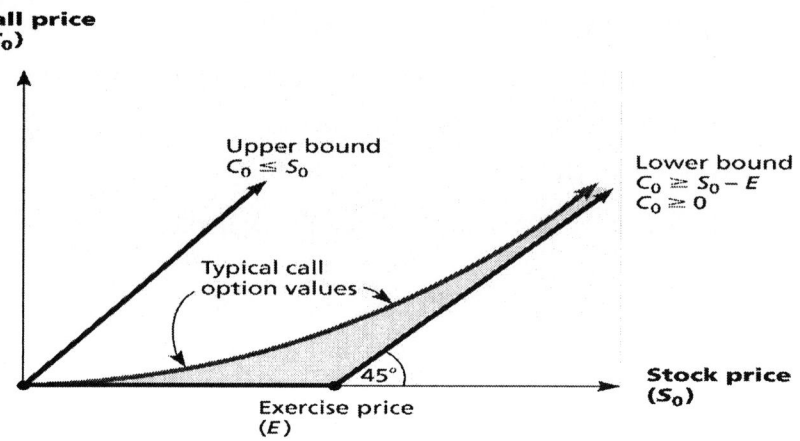

As shown, the upper bound on a call's value is given by the value of the stock ($C_0 \leq S_0$). The lower bound is either $S_0 - E$ or zero, whichever is larger. The highlighted curve illustrates the value of a call option prior to maturity for different stock prices.

A Simple Model

- An option is "in-the-money" if the payoff is greater than zero
- *If* a call option is sure to finish in-the-money, the option value would be
  - $C_0 = S_0 - PV(E)$
- If the call is worth something other than this, then there is an arbitrage opportunity

14.11 What Determines Option Values?

- Stock price
  - As the stock price increases, the call price increases and the put price decreases
- Exercise price
  - As the exercise price increases, the call price decreases and the put price increases
- Time to expiration
  - Generally, as the time to expiration increases both the call and the put prices increase
- Risk-free rate
  - As the risk-free rate increases, the call price increases and the put price decreases

14.12 What about Variance?

- When an option may finish out-of-the-money (expire without being exercised), there is another factor that helps determine price
- The variance in underlying asset returns is a less obvious, but important, determinant of option values
- The greater the variance, the more the call and the put are worth
  - If an option finishes out-of-the-money, the most you can lose is your premium, no matter how far out it is
  - The more an option is in-the-money, the greater the gain
  - You gain from volatility on the upside, but don't lose anymore from volatility on the downside

Table 14.2

Factor	Direction of Influence	
	Calls	Puts
Current value of the underlying asset	(+)	(−)
Exercise price on the option	(−)	(+)
Time to expiration on the option	(+)	(+)
Risk-free rate	(+)	(−)
Variance of return on the underlying asset	(+)	(+)

Employee Stock Options

- Options that are given to employees as part of their benefits package
- Often used as a bonus or incentive
  - Designed to align employee interests with stockholder interests and reduce agency problems
  - Empirical evidence suggests that they don't work as well as anticipated due to the lack of diversification introduced into the employees' portfolios
  - The stock just isn't worth as much to the employee as it is to an outside investor

14.15 Equity: A Call Option

- Equity can be viewed as a call option on the company's assets when the firm is leveraged
- The exercise price is the value of the debt
- If the assets are worth more than the debt when it comes due, the option will be exercised and the stockholders retain ownership
- If the assets are worth less than the debt, the stockholders will let the option expire and the assets will belong to the bondholders

14.16 Capital Budgeting Options

- Almost all capital budgeting scenarios contain implicit options
- Because options are valuable, they make the capital budgeting project worth more than it may appear
- Failure to account for these options can cause firms to reject good projects

14.17 Timing Options

- We normally assume that a project must be taken today or foregone completely
- Almost all projects have the embedded option to wait
  - A good project may be worth more if we wait
  - A seemly bad project may actually have a positive NPV if we wait due to changing economic conditions
- We should examine the NPV of taking an investment now, or in future years, and plan to invest at the time that produces the highest NPV

14.18 Example: Timing Options

- Consider a project that costs $5000 and has an expected future cash flow of $700 per year forever. If we wait one year, the cost will increase to $5500 and the expected future cash flow increase to $750. If the required return is 13%, should we accept the project? If so, when should we begin?
  - NPV starting today = -5000 + 700/.13 = 384.16
  - NPV waiting one year = (-5500 + 800/.13)/(1.13) = 578.62
  - It is a good project either way, but we should wait until next year

14.19 Managerial Options

- Managers often have options after a project has been implemented that can add value
- It is important to do some contingency planning ahead of time to determine what will cause the options to be exercised
- Some examples include
  - The option to expand a project if it goes well
  - The option to abandon a project if it goes poorly
  - The option to suspend or contract operations particularly in the manufacturing industries
  - Strategic options – look at how taking this project opens up other opportunities that would be otherwise unavailable

14.20 Warrants

- A call option issued by corporations in conjunction with other securities to reduce the yield
- Differences between warrants and traditional call options
  - Warrants are generally very long term
  - They are written by the company and exercise results in additional shares outstanding
  - The exercise price is paid to the company and generates cash for the firm
  - Warrants can be detached from the original securities and sold separately

14.21 Convertibles

- Convertible bonds (or preferred stock) may be converted into a specified number of common shares at the option of the bondholder
- The conversion price is the effective price paid for the stock
- The conversion ratio is the number of shares received when the bond is converted
- Convertible bonds will be worth at least as much as the straight bond value or the conversion value, whichever is greater

14.22 Valuing Convertibles

- Suppose you have a 10% bond that pays semiannual coupons and will mature in 15 years. The face value is $1000 and the yield to maturity on similar bonds is 9%. The bond is also convertible with a conversion price of $100. The stock is currently selling for $110. What is the minimum price of the bond?
    - Straight bond value = 1081.44
    - Conversion ratio = 1000/100 = 10
    - Conversion value = 10*110 = 1100
    - Minimum price = $1100

14.23 Other Options

- Call provision on a bond
  - Allows the company to repurchase the bond prior to maturity at a specified price that is generally higher than the face value
  - Increases the required yield on the bond – this is effectively how the company pays for the option
- Put bond
  - Allows the bondholder to require the company to repurchase the bond prior to maturity at a fixed price
- Insurance and Loan Guarantees
  - These are essentially put options

14.24 Quick Quiz

- What is the difference between a call option and a put option?
- What is the intrinsic value of call and put options and what do the payoff diagrams look like?
- What are the five major determinants of option prices and their relationships to option prices?
- What are some of the major capital budgeting options?
- How would you value a convertible bond?

15.1 Key Concepts and Skills

- Know how to determine a firm's cost of equity capital
- Know how to determine a firm's cost of debt
- Know how to determine a firm's overall cost of capital
- Understand pitfalls of overall cost of capital and how to manage them

15.2 Chapter Outline

- The Cost of Capital: Some Preliminaries
- The Cost of Equity
- The Costs of Debt and Preferred Stock
- The Weighted Average Cost of Capital
- Divisional and Project Costs of Capital
- Flotation Costs and the Weighted Average Cost of Capital

15.3 Why Cost of Capital Is Important

- We know that the return earned on assets depends on the risk of those assets
- The return to an investor is the same as the cost to the company
- Our cost of capital provides us with an indication of how the market views the risk of our assets
- Knowing our cost of capital can also help us determine our required return for capital budgeting projects

15.4 Required Return

- The required return is the same as the appropriate discount rate and is based on the risk of the cash flows
- We need to know the required return for an investment before we can compute the NPV and make a decision about whether or not to take the investment
- We need to earn at least the required return to compensate our investors for the financing they have provided

15.5 Cost of Equity

- The cost of equity is the return required by equity investors given the risk of the cash flows from the firm
- There are two major methods for determining the cost of equity
  - Dividend growth model
  - SML or CAPM

15.6 The Dividend Growth Model Approach

- Start with the dividend growth model formula and rearrange to solve for R_E

$$P_0 = \frac{D_1}{R_E - g}$$

$$R_E = \frac{D_1}{P_0} + g$$

15.7 Dividend Growth Model Example

- Suppose that your company is expected to pay a dividend of $1.50 per share next year. There has been a steady growth in dividends of 5.1% per year and the market expects that to continue. The current price is $25. What is the cost of equity?

$$R_E = \frac{1.50}{25} + .051 = .111$$

15.8 Example: Estimating the Dividend Growth Rate

- One method for estimating the growth rate is to use the historical average

Year	Dividend	Percent Change
1995	1.23	
1996	1.30	(1.30 – 1.23) / 1.23 = 5.7%
1997	1.36	(1.36 – 1.30) / 1.30 = 4.6%
1998	1.43	(1.43 – 1.36) / 1.36 = 5.1%
1999	1.50	(1.50 – 1.43) / 1.43 = 4.9%

  Average = (5.7 + 4.6 + 5.1 + 4.9) / 4 = 5.1%

15.9 Advantages and Disadvantages of Dividend Growth Model

- Advantage – easy to understand and use
- Disadvantages
  - Only applicable to companies currently paying dividends
  - Not applicable if dividends aren't growing at a reasonably constant rate
  - Extremely sensitive to the estimated growth rate – an increase in g of 1% increases the cost of equity by 1%
  - Does not explicitly consider risk

15.10 The SML Approach

- Use the following information to compute our cost of equity
  - Risk-free rate, R_f
  - Market risk premium, $E(R_M) - R_f$
  - Systematic risk of asset, β

$$R_E = R_f + \beta_E(E(R_M) - R_f)$$

15.11 Example - SML

- Suppose your company has an equity beta of .58 and the current risk-free rate is 6.1%. If the expected market risk premium is 8.6%, what is your cost of equity capital?
  - $R_E = 6.1 + .58(8.6) = 11.1\%$
- Since we came up with similar numbers using both the dividend growth model and the SML approach, we should feel pretty good about our estimate

15.12 Advantages and Disadvantages of SML

- Advantages
  - Explicitly adjusts for systematic risk
  - Applicable to all companies, as long as we can compute beta
- Disadvantages
  - Have to estimate the *expected* market risk premium, which does vary over time
  - Have to estimate beta, which also varies over time
  - We are relying on the past to predict the future, which is not always reliable

Example – Cost of Equity

- Suppose our company has a beta of 1.5. The market risk premium is expected to be 9% and the current risk-free rate is 6%. We have used analysts' estimates to determine that the market believes our dividends will grow at 6% per year and our last dividend was $2. Our stock is currently selling for $15.65. What is our cost of equity?
    - Using SML: $R_E = 6\% + 1.5(9\%) = 19.5\%$
    - Using DGM: $R_E = [2(1.06) / 15.65] + .06 = 19.55\%$

Cost of Debt

- The cost of debt is the required return on our company's debt
- We usually focus on the cost of long-term debt or bonds
- The required return is best estimated by computing the yield-to-maturity on the existing debt
- We may also use estimates of current rates based on the bond rating we expect when we issue new debt
- The cost of debt is NOT the coupon rate

15.15 Example: Cost of Debt

- Suppose we have a bond issue currently outstanding that has 25 years left to maturity. The coupon rate is 9% and coupons are paid semiannually. The bond is currently selling for $908.72 per $1000 bond. What is the cost of debt?
  - N = 50; PMT = 45; FV = 1000; PV = -908.75; CPT I/Y = 5%; YTM = 5(2) = 10%

15.16 Cost of Preferred Stock

- Reminders
  - Preferred generally pays a constant dividend every period
  - Dividends are expected to be paid every period forever
- Preferred stock is an annuity, so we take the annuity formula, rearrange and solve for R_P
- $R_P = D / P_0$

Example: Cost of Preferred Stock

- Your company has preferred stock that has an annual dividend of $3. If the current price is $25, what is the cost of preferred stock?
- $R_P = 3 / 25 = 12\%$

The Weighted Average Cost of Capital

- We can use the individual costs of capital that we have computed to get our "average" cost of capital for the firm.
- This "average" is the required return on our assets, based on the market's perception of the risk of those assets
- The weights are determined by how much of each type of financing that we use

15.19 Capital Structure Weights

- Notation
  - E = market value of equity = # outstanding shares times price per share
  - D = market value of debt = # outstanding bonds times bond price
  - V = market value of the firm = D + E
- Weights
  - w_E = E/V = percent financed with equity
  - w_D = D/V = percent financed with debt

15.20 Example: Capital Structure Weights

- Suppose you have a market value of equity equal to $500 million and a market value of debt = $475 million.
  - What are the capital structure weights?
    - V = 500 million + 475 million = 975 million
    - w_E = E/D = 500 / 975 = .5128 = 51.28%
    - w_D = D/V = 475 / 975 = .4872 = 48.72%

15.21 Taxes and the WACC

- We are concerned with after-tax cash flows, so we need to consider the effect of taxes on the various costs of capital
- Interest expense reduces our tax liability
  - This reduction in taxes reduces our cost of debt
  - After-tax cost of debt = $R_D(1-T_C)$
- Dividends are not tax deductible, so there is no tax impact on the cost of equity
- WACC = $w_E R_E + w_D R_D(1-T_C)$

15.22 Extended Example – WACC - I

- Equity Information
  - 50 million shares
  - $80 per share
  - Beta = 1.15
  - Market risk premium = 9%
  - Risk-free rate = 5%
- Debt Information
  - $1 billion in outstanding debt (face value)
  - Current quote = 110
  - Coupon rate = 9%, semiannual coupons
  - 15 years to maturity
- Tax rate = 40%

15.23 Extended Example – WACC - II

- What is the cost of equity?
  - $R_E = 5 + 1.15(9) = 15.35\%$
- What is the cost of debt?
  - N = 30; PV = -1100; PMT = 45; FV = 1000; CPT I/Y = 3.9268
  - $R_D = 3.927(2) = 7.854\%$
- What is the after-tax cost of debt?
  - $R_D(1-T_C) = 7.854(1-.4) = 4.712\%$

15.24 Extended Example – WACC - III

- What are the capital structure weights?
  - E = 50 million (80) = 4 billion
  - D = 1 billion (1.10) = 1.1 billion
  - V = 4 + 1.1 = 5.1 billion
  - w_E = E/V = 4 / 5.1 = .7843
  - w_D = D/V = 1.1 / 5.1 = .2157
- What is the WACC?
  - WACC = .7843(15.35%) + .2157(4.712%) = 13.06%

15.25 Eastman Chemical I

- Click on the web surfer to go to Yahoo Finance to get information on Eastman Chemical (EMN)
- Under profile, you can find the following information
  - # shares outstanding
  - Book value per share
  - Price per share
  - Beta
- Under research, you can find analysts estimates of earnings growth (use as a proxy for dividend growth)
- The bonds section at Yahoo Finance can provide the T-bill rate
- Use this information, along with the CAPM and DGM to estimate the cost of equity

15.26 Eastman Chemical II

- Go to Bondsonline to get market information on Eastman Chemical's bond issues
  - Enter Eastman Ch to find the bond information
  - Note that you may not be able to find information on all bond issues due to the illiquidity of the bond market
- Go to the SEC site to get book market information from the firm's most recent 10Q

15.27 Eastman Chemical III

- Find the weighted average cost of the debt
  - Use market values if you were able to get the information
  - Use the book values if market information was not available
  - They are often very close
- Compute the WACC
  - Use market value weights if available

15.28 Table 15.1 Cost of Equity

I. The cost of equity, R_E

A. Dividend growth model approach (from Chapter 8):

$$R_E = D_1/P_0 + g$$

where D_1 is the expected dividend in one period, g is the dividend growth rate, and P_0 is the current stock price.

B. SML approach (from Chapter 13):

$$R_E = R_f + \beta_E \times (R_M - R_f)$$

where R_f is the risk-free rate, R_M is the expected return on the overall market, and β_E is the systematic risk of the equity.

Table 15.1 Cost of Debt

II. The cost of debt, R_D

  A. For a firm with publicly held debt, the cost of debt can be measured as the yield to maturity on the outstanding debt. The coupon rate is irrelevant. Yield to maturity is covered in Chapter 7.

  B. If the firm has no publicly traded debt, then the cost of debt can be measured as the yield to maturity on similarly rated bonds (bond ratings are discussed in Chapter 7).

Table 15.1 WACC

III. The weighted average cost of capital, WACC

  A. The firm's WACC is the overall required return on the firm as a whole. It is the appropriate discount rate to use for cash flows similar in risk to those of the overall firm.

  B. The WACC is calculated as:

  $$WACC = (E/V) \times R_E + (D/V) \times R_D \times (1 - T_C)$$

  where T_C is the corporate tax rate, E is the *market* value of the firm's equity, D is the *market* value of the firm's debt, and $V = E + D$. Note that E/V is the percentage of the firm's financing (in market value terms) that is equity, and D/V is the percentage that is debt.

15.31 Divisional and Project Costs of Capital

- Using the WACC as our discount rate is only appropriate for projects that are the same risk as the firm's current operations
- If we are looking at a project that is NOT the same risk as the firm, then we need to determine the appropriate discount rate for that project
- Divisions also often require separate discount rates

15.32 Using WACC for All Projects - Example

- What would happen if we use the WACC for all projects regardless of risk?
- Assume the WACC = 15%

Project	Required Return	IRR
A	20%	17%
B	15%	18%
C	10%	12%

15.33 The Pure Play Approach

- Find one or more companies that specialize in the product or service that we are considering
- Compute the beta for each company
- Take an average
- Use that beta along with the CAPM to find the appropriate return for a project of that risk
- Often difficult to find pure play companies

15.34 Subjective Approach

- Consider the project's risk relative to the firm overall
- If the project is more risky than the firm, use a discount rate greater than the WACC
- If the project is less risky than the firm, use a discount rate less than the WACC
- You may still accept projects that you shouldn't and reject projects you should accept, but your error rate should be lower than not considering differential risk at all

Subjective Approach - Example

Risk Level	Discount Rate
Very Low Risk	WACC – 8%
Low Risk	WACC – 3%
Same Risk as Firm	WACC
High Risk	WACC + 5%
Very High Risk	WACC + 10%

Flotation Costs

- The required return depends on the risk, not how the money is raised
- However, the cost of issuing new securities should not just be ignored either
- Basic Approach
    - Compute the weighted average flotation cost
    - Use the target weights because the firm will issue securities in these percentages over the long term

15.37 NPV and Flotation Costs - Example

- Your company is considering a project that will cost $1 million. The project will generate after-tax cash flows of $250,000 per year for 7 years. The WACC is 15% and the firm's target D/E ratio is .6 The flotation cost for equity is 5% and the flotation cost for debt is 3%. What is the NPV for the project after adjusting for flotation costs?
  - f_A = (.375)(3%) + (.625)(5%) = 4.25%
  - PV of future cash flows = 1,040,105
  - NPV = 1,040,105 - 1,000,000/(1-.0425) = -4,281
- The project would have a positive NPV of 40,105 without considering flotation costs
- Once we consider the cost of issuing new securities, the NPV becomes negative

15.38 Quick Quiz

- What are the two approaches for computing the cost of equity?
- How do you compute the cost of debt and the after-tax cost of debt?
- How do you compute the capital structure weights required for the WACC?
- What is the WACC?
- What happens if we use the WACC for the discount rate for all projects?
- What are two methods that can be used to compute the appropriate discount rate when WACC isn't appropriate?
- How should we factor in flotation costs to our analysis?

16.1 Key Concepts and Skills

- Understand the venture capital market and its role in financing new businesses
- Understand how securities are sold to the public and the role of investment bankers
- Understand initial public offerings and the costs of going public

16.2 Chapter Outline

- The Financing Life Cycle of a Firm: Early-Stage Financing and Venture Capital
- Selling Securities to the Public: The Basic Procedure
- Alternative Issue Methods
- Underwriters
- IPOs and Underpricing
- New Equity Sales and the Value of the Firm
- The Cost of Issuing Securities
- Rights
- Dilution
- Issuing Long-Term Debt
- Shelf Registration

16.3 Venture Capital

- Private financing for relatively new businesses in exchange for stock
- Usually entails some hands-on guidance
- The ultimate goal is usually to take the company public and the VC will benefit from the capital raised in the IPO
- Many VC firms are formed from a group of investors that pool capital and then have partners in the firm decide which companies will receive financing
- Some large corporations have a VC division

16.4 Choosing a Venture Capitalist

- Look for financial strength
- Choose a VC that has a management style that is compatible with your own
- Obtain and check references
- What contacts does the VC have?
- What is the exit strategy?

16.5 Selling Securities to the Public

- Management must obtain permission from the Board of Directors
- Firm must file a registration statement with the SEC
- SEC examines the registration during a 20-day waiting period
    - A preliminary prospectus, called a red herring, is distributed during the waiting period
    - If there are problems the company is allowed to amend the registration and the waiting period starts over
- Securities may not be sold during the waiting period
- The price is determined on the effective date of the registration

16.6 Table 16.1 - I

Method	Type	Definition
Public Traditional negotiated cash offer	Firm commitment cash offer	Company negotiates an agreement with an investment banker to underwrite and distribute the new shares. A specified number of shares are bought by underwriters and sold at a higher price.
	Best efforts cash offer	Company has investment bankers sell as many of the new shares as possible at the agreed-upon price. There is no guarantee concerning how much cash will be raised.
Privileged subscription	Direct rights offer	Company offers the new stock directly to its existing shareholders.
	Standby rights offer	Like the direct rights offer, this contains a privileged subscription arrangement with existing shareholders. The net proceeds are guaranteed by the underwriters.

Table 16.1 - II

Nontraditional cash offer	Shelf cash offer	Qualifying companies can authorize all shares they expect to sell over a two-year period and sell them when needed.
	Competitive firm cash offer	Company can elect to award the underwriting contract through a public auction instead of negotiation.
Private	Direct placement	Securities are sold directly to the purchaser, who, at least until recently, generally could not resell securities for at least two years.

Underwriters

- Services provided by underwriters
  - Formulate method used to issue securities
  - Price the securities
  - Sell the securities
  - Price stabilization by lead underwriter
- Syndicate – group of investment bankers that market the securities and share the risk associated with selling the issue
- Spread – difference between what the syndicate pays the company and what the security sells for in the market

16.9 Firm Commitment Underwriting

- Issuer sells entire issue to underwriting syndicate
- The syndicate then resells the issue to the public
- The underwriter makes money on the spread between the price paid to the issuer and the price received from investors when the stock is sold
- The syndicate bears the risk of not being able to sell the entire issue for more than the cost
- Most common type of underwriting in the United States

16.10 Best Efforts Underwriting

- Underwriter must make their "best effort" to sell the securities at an agreed-upon offering price
- The company bears the risk of the issue not being sold
- The offer may be pulled if there is not enough interest at the offer price and the company does not get the capital and they have still incurred substantial flotation costs
- Not as common as it used to be

16.11 Green Shoes and Lockups

- Green Shoe provision
  - Allows syndicate to purchase an additional 15% of the issue from the issuer
  - Allows the issue to be oversubscribed
  - Provides some protection for the lead underwriter as they perform their price stabilization function
- Lockup agreements
  - Restriction on insiders that prevents them from selling their shares of an IPO for a specified time period
  - The lockup period is commonly 180 days
  - The stock price tends to drop when the lockup period expires due to market anticipation of additional shares hitting the street

16.12 IPO Underpricing

- Initial Public Offering – IPO
- May be difficult to price an IPO because there isn't a current market price available
- Additional asymmetric information associated with companies going public
- Underwriters want to ensure that their clients earn a good return on IPOs on average
- Underpricing causes the issuer to "leave money on the table"

16.13 Figure 16.2

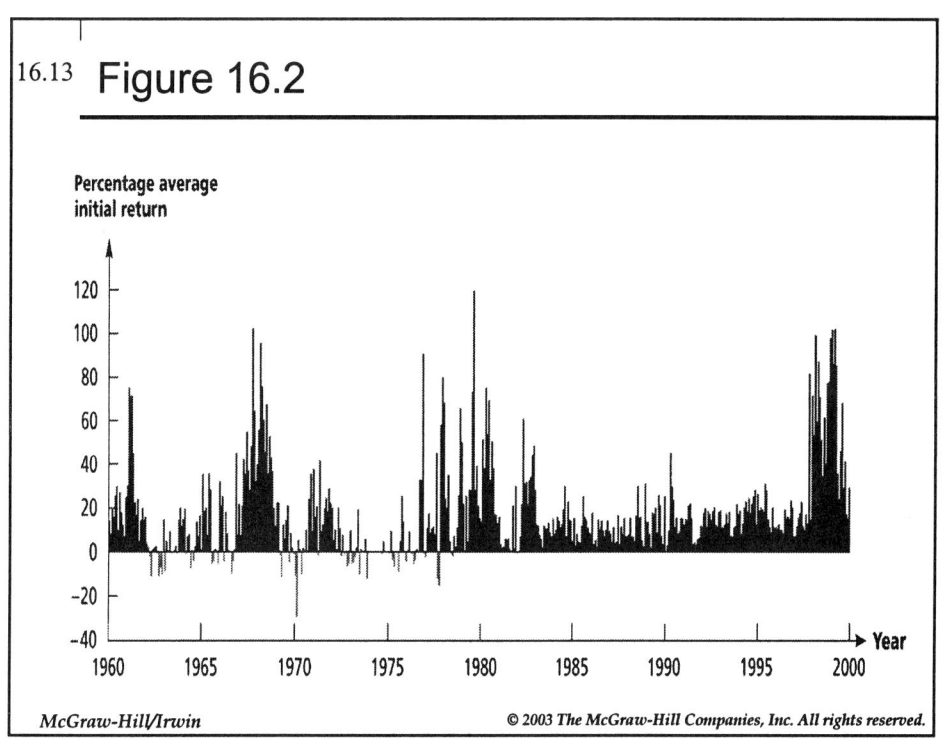

16.14 Figure 16.3

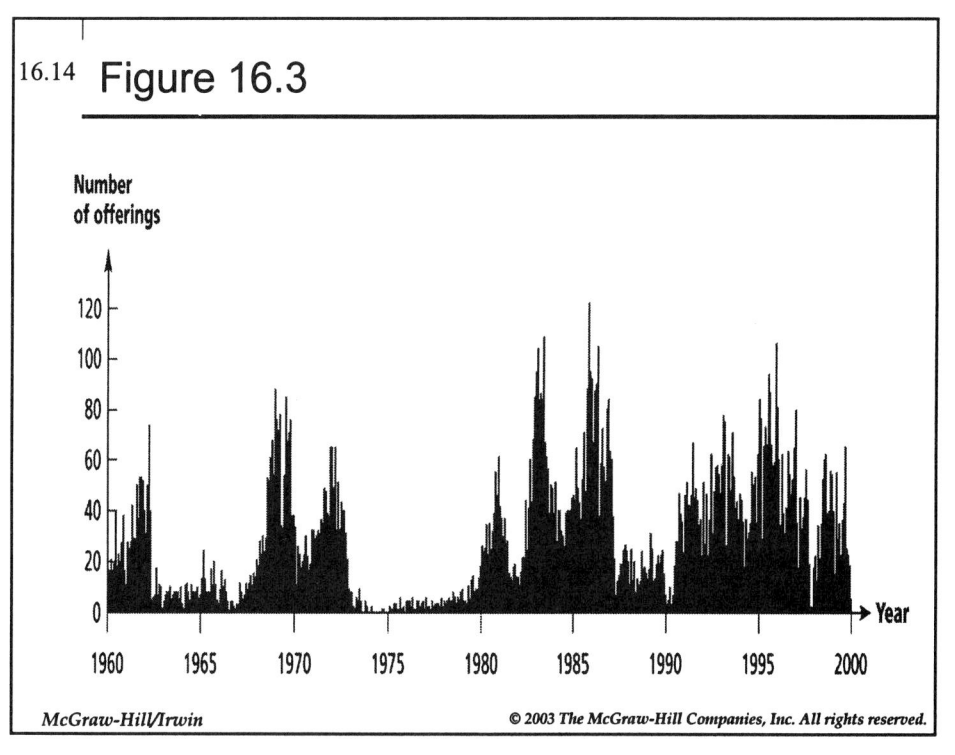

16.15 Work the Web Example

- How have recent IPOs done?
- Click on the web surfer to go to the Bloomberg site and follow the "IPO Center" link
  - How many companies have gone public in the last week?
  - How have companies that went public three months ago done? What about six months ago?

16.16 New Equity Issues and Price

- Stock prices tend to decline when new equity is issued
- Possible explanations for this phenomenon
  - Signaling and managerial information
  - Signaling and debt usage
  - Issue costs
- Since the drop in price can be significant and much of the drop may be attributable to negative signals, it is important for management to understand the signals that are being sent and try to reduce the effect when possible

16.17 Issuance Costs

- Spread
- Other direct expenses – legal fees, filing fees, etc.
- Indirect expenses – opportunity costs, i.e., management time spent working on issue
- Abnormal returns – price drop on existing stock
- Underpricing – below market issue price on IPOs
- Green Shoe option – cost of additional shares that the syndicate can purchase after the issue has gone to market

16.18 Rights Offerings: Basic Concepts

- Issue of common stock offered to existing shareholders
- Allows current shareholders to avoid the dilution that can occur with a new stock issue
- "Rights" are given to the shareholders
  - Specify number of shares that can be purchased
  - Specify purchase price
  - Specify time frame
- Rights may be traded OTC or on an exchange

16.19 The Value of a Right

- The price specified in a rights offering is generally less than the current market price
- The share price will adjust based on the number of new shares issued
- The value of the right is the difference between the old share price and the "new" share price

16.20 Rights Offering Example

- Suppose a company wants to raise $10 million. The subscription price is $20 and the current stock price is $25. The firm currently has 5,000,000 shares outstanding.
    - How many shares have to be issued?
    - How many rights will it take to purchase one share?
    - What is the value of a right?

More on Rights Offerings

- Ex-rights – the price of the stock will drop by the value of the right on the day that the stock no longer carries the "right"
- Standby underwriting – underwriter agrees to buy any shares that are not purchased through the rights offering
- Stockholders can either exercise their rights or sell them – they are not hurt by the rights offering either way
- Rights offerings are generally cheaper, yet they are much less common than general cash offers in the U.S.

Dilution

- Dilution is a loss in value for existing shareholders
  - Percentage ownership – shares sold to the general public without a rights offering
  - Market value – firm accepts negative NPV projects
  - Book value and EPS – occurs when market-to-book value is less than one

16.23 Types of Long-term Debt

- Bonds – public issue of long-term debt
- Private issues
  - Term loans
    - Direct business loans from commercial banks, insurance companies, etc.
    - Maturities 1 – 5 years
    - Repayable during life of the loan
  - Private placements
    - Similar to term loans with longer maturity
  - Easier to renegotiate than public issues
  - Lower costs than public issues

16.24 Shelf Registration

- Permits a corporation to register a large issue with the SEC and sell it in small portions
- Reduces the flotation costs of registration
- Allows the company more flexibility to raise money quickly
- Requirements
  - Company must be rated investment grade
  - Cannot have defaulted on debt within last three years
  - Market value of stock must be greater than $150 million
  - No violations of the Securities Act of 1934 in the last three years

16.25 Quick Quiz

- What is venture capital and what types of firms receive it?
- What are some of the important services provided by underwriters?
- What type of underwriting is the most common in the United States and how does it work?
- What is IPO underpricing and why might it persist?
- What are some of the costs associated with issuing securities?
- What is a rights offering and how do you value a right?
- What are some of the characteristics of private placement debt?
- What is shelf registration?

17.1 Key Concepts and Skills

- Understand the effect of financial leverage on cash flows and cost of equity
- Understand the impact of taxes and bankruptcy on capital structure choice
- Understand the basic components of the bankruptcy process

17.2 Chapter Outline

- The Capital Structure Question
- The Effect of Financial Leverage
- Capital Structure and the Cost of Equity Capital
- M&M Propositions I and II with Corporate Taxes
- Bankruptcy Costs
- Optimal Capital Structure
- The Pie Again
- Observed Capital Structures
- A Quick Look at the Bankruptcy Process

17.3 Capital Restructuring

- We are going to look at how changes in capital structure affect the value of the firm, *all else equal*
- Capital restructuring involves changing the amount of leverage a firm has without changing the firm's assets
- Increase leverage by issuing debt and repurchasing outstanding shares
- Decrease leverage by issuing new shares and retiring outstanding debt

17.4 Choosing a Capital Structure

- What is the primary goal of financial managers?
  - Maximize stockholder wealth
- We want to choose the capital structure that will maximize stockholder wealth
- We can maximize stockholder wealth by maximizing firm value or minimizing WACC

17.5 The Effect of Leverage

- How does leverage affect the EPS and ROE of a firm?
- When we increase the amount of debt financing, we increase the fixed interest expense
- If we have a really good year, then we pay our fixed cost and we have more left over for our stockholders
- If we have a really bad year, we still have to pay our fixed costs and we have less left over for our stockholders
- Leverage amplifies the variation in both EPS and ROE

17.6 Example: Financial Leverage, EPS and ROE

- We will ignore the effect of taxes at this stage
- What happens to EPS and ROE when we issue debt and buy back shares of stock?

Financial Leverage Example

17.7 Example: Financial Leverage, EPS and ROE

- Variability in ROE
  - Current: ROE ranges from 6.25% to 18.75%
  - Proposed: ROE ranges from 2.50% to 27.50%
- Variability in EPS
  - Current: EPS ranges from $1.25 to $3.75
  - Proposed: EPS ranges from $0.50 to $5.50
- The variability in both ROE and EPS increases when financial leverage is increased

17.8 Break-Even EBIT

- Find EBIT where EPS is the same under both the current and proposed capital structures
- If we expect EBIT to be greater than the break-even point, then leverage is beneficial to our stockholders
- If we expect EBIT to be less than the break-even point, then leverage is detrimental to our stockholders

17.9 Example: Break-Even EBIT

$$\frac{\text{EBIT}}{400{,}000} = \frac{\text{EBIT} - 400{,}000}{200{,}000}$$

$$\text{EBIT} = \left[\frac{400{,}000}{200{,}000}\right](\text{EBIT} - 400{,}000)$$

$$\text{EBIT} = 2\,\text{EBIT} - 800{,}000$$

$$\text{EBIT} = \$800{,}000$$

$$\text{EPS} = \frac{800{,}000}{400{,}000} = \$2.00$$

Break-even Graph

17.10 Example: Homemade Leverage and ROE

- **Current Capital Structure**
  - Investor borrows $2000 and uses $2000 of their own to buy 200 shares of stock
  - Payoffs:
    - Recession: 200(1.25) - .1(2000) = $50
    - Expected: 200(2.50) - .1(2000) = $300
    - Expansion: 200(3.75) - .1(2000) = $550
  - Mirrors the payoffs from purchasing 100 shares from the firm under the proposed capital structure

- **Proposed Capital Structure**
  - Investor buys $1000 worth of stock (50 shares) and $1000 worth of Trans Am bonds paying 10%.
  - Payoffs:
    - Recession: 50(.50) + .1(1000) = $125
    - Expected: 50(3.00) + .1(1000) = $250
    - Expansion: 50(5.50) + .1(1000) = $375
  - Mirrors the payoffs from purchasing 100 shares under the current capital structure

17.11 Capital Structure Theory

- Modigliani and Miller Theory of Capital Structure
  - Proposition I – firm value
  - Proposition II – WACC
- The value of the firm is determined by the cash flows to the firm and the risk of the assets
- Changing firm value
  - Change the risk of the cash flows
  - Change the cash flows

17.12 Capital Structure Theory Under Three Special Cases

- Case I – Assumptions
  - No corporate or personal taxes
  - No bankruptcy costs
- Case II – Assumptions
  - Corporate taxes, but no personal taxes
  - No bankruptcy costs
- Case III – Assumptions
  - Corporate taxes, but no personal taxes
  - Bankruptcy costs

17.13 Case I – Propositions I and II

- Proposition I
  - The value of the firm is NOT affected by changes in the capital structure
  - The cash flows of the firm do not change, therefore value doesn't change
- Proposition II
  - The WACC of the firm is NOT affected by capital structure

17.14 Case I - Equations

- $WACC = R_A = (E/V)R_E + (D/V)R_D$

- $R_E = R_A + (R_A - R_D)(D/E)$

  - R_A is the "cost" of the firm's business risk, i.e., the risk of the firm's assets
  - $(R_A - R_D)(D/E)$ is the "cost" of the firm's financial risk, i.e., the additional return required by stockholders to compensate for the risk of leverage

Figure 17.3

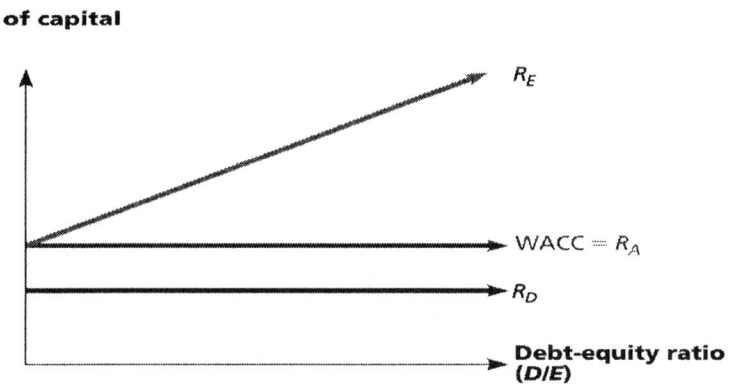

$R_E = R_A + (R_A - R_D) \times (D/E)$ by M&M Proposition II
$R_A = WACC = \left(\dfrac{E}{V}\right) \times R_E + \left(\dfrac{D}{V}\right) \times R_D$
where $V = D + E$

Case I - Example

- Data
  - Required return on assets = 16%, cost of debt = 10%; percent of debt = 45%
- What is the cost of equity?
  - $R_E = .16 + (.16 - .10)(.45/.55) = .2091 = 20.91\%$
- Suppose instead that the cost of equity is 25%, what is the debt-to-equity ratio?
  - $.25 = .16 + (.16 - .10)(D/E)$
  - $D/E = (.25 - .16) / (.16 - .10) = 1.5$
- Based on this information, what is the percent of equity in the firm?
  - $E/V = 1 / 2.5 = 40\%$

17.17 The CAPM, the SML and Proposition II

- How does financial leverage affect systematic risk?
- CAPM: $R_A = R_f + \beta_A(R_M - R_f)$
  - Where β_A is the firm's asset beta and measures the systematic risk of the firm's assets
- Proposition II
  - Replace R_A with the CAPM and assume that the debt is riskless ($R_D = R_f$)
  - $R_E = R_f + \beta_A(1+D/E)(R_M - R_f)$

17.18 Business Risk and Financial Risk

- $R_E = R_f + \beta_A(1+D/E)(R_M - R_f)$
- CAPM: $R_E = R_f + \beta_E(R_M - R_f)$
  - $\beta_E = \beta_A(1 + D/E)$
- Therefore, the systematic risk of the stock depends on:
  - Systematic risk of the assets, β_A, (Business risk)
  - Level of leverage, D/E, (Financial risk)

17.19 Case II – Cash Flow

- Interest is tax deductible
- Therefore, when a firm adds debt, it reduces taxes, all else equal
- The reduction in taxes increases the cash flow of the firm
- How should an increase in cash flows affect the value of the firm?

17.20 Case II - Example

	Unlevered Firm	Levered Firm
EBIT	5000	5000
Interest	0	500
Taxable Income	5000	4500
Taxes (34%)	1700	1530
Net Income	3300	2970
CFFA	3300	3470

17.21 Interest Tax Shield

- Annual interest tax shield
  - Tax rate times interest payment
  - 6250 in 8% debt = 500 in interest expense
  - Annual tax shield = .34(500) = 170
- Present value of annual interest tax shield
  - Assume perpetual debt for simplicity
  - PV = 170 / .08 = 2125
  - PV = $D(R_D)(T_C) / R_D = DT_C$ = 6250(.34) = 2125

17.22 Case II – Proposition I

- The value of the firm increases by the present value of the annual interest tax shield
  - Value of a levered firm = value of an unlevered firm + PV of interest tax shield
  - Value of equity = Value of the firm – Value of debt
- Assuming perpetual cash flows
  - V_U = EBIT(1-T) / R_U
  - $V_L = V_U + DT_C$

Example: Case II – Proposition I

- Data
  - EBIT = 25 million; Tax rate = 35%; Debt = $75 million; Cost of debt = 9%; Unlevered cost of capital = 12%
- $V_U = 25(1-.35) / .12 = \$135.42$ million
- $V_L = 135.42 + 75(.35) = \$161.67$ million
- $E = 161.67 - 75 = \$86.67$ million

Figure 17.4

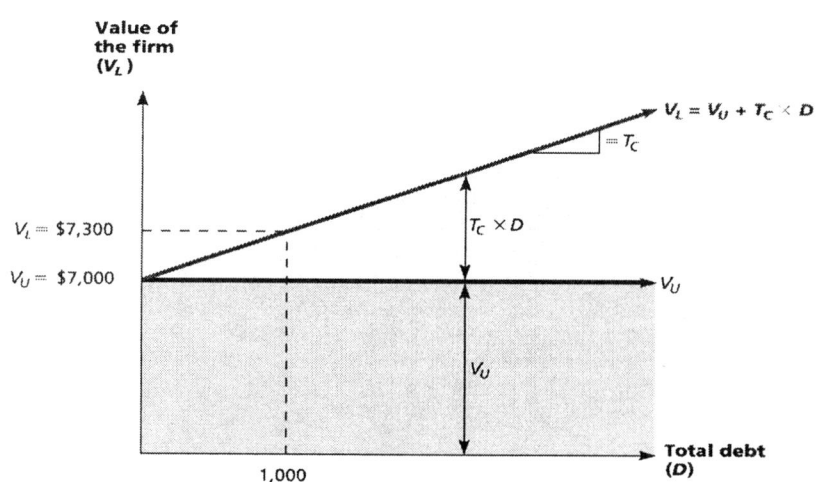

The value of the firm increases as total debt increases because of the interest tax shield. This is the basis of M&M Proposition I with taxes.

Case II – Proposition II

- The WACC decreases as D/E increases because of the government subsidy on interest payments
  - $R_A = (E/V)R_E + (D/V)(R_D)(1-T_C)$
  - $R_E = R_U + (R_U - R_D)(D/E)(1-T_C)$
- Example
  - $R_E = .12 + (.12-.09)(75/86.67)(1-.35) = 13.69\%$
  - $R_A = (86.67/161.67)(.1369) + (75/161.67)(.09)(1-.35)$
    $R_A = 10.05\%$

Example: Case II – Proposition II

- Suppose that the firm changes its capital structure so that the debt-to-equity ratio becomes 1.
- What will happen to the cost of equity under the new capital structure?
  - $R_E = .12 + (.12 - .09)(1)(1-.35) = 13.95\%$
- What will happen to the weighted average cost of capital?
  - $R_A = .5(.1395) + .5(.09)(1-.35) = 9.9\%$

Figure 17.5

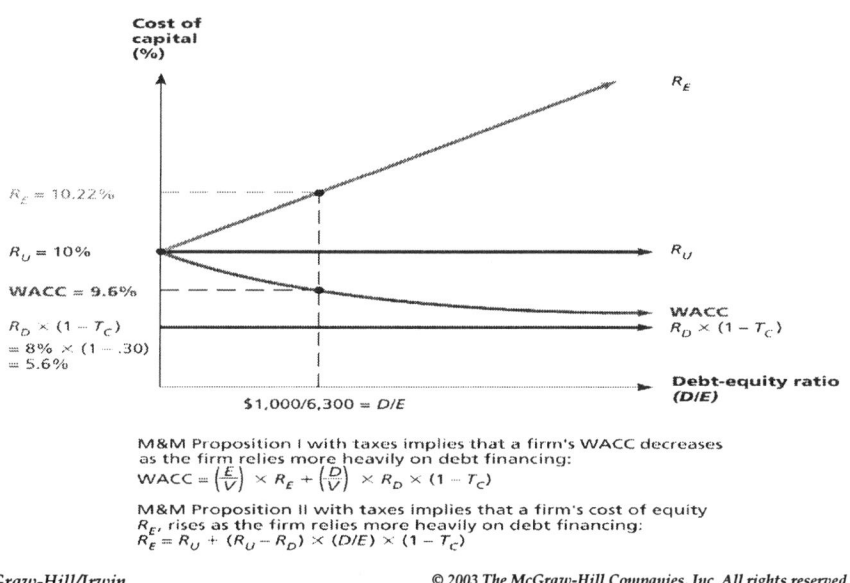

M&M Proposition I with taxes implies that a firm's WACC decreases as the firm relies more heavily on debt financing:
$$WACC = \left(\frac{E}{V}\right) \times R_E + \left(\frac{D}{V}\right) \times R_D \times (1 - T_C)$$

M&M Proposition II with taxes implies that a firm's cost of equity R_E, rises as the firm relies more heavily on debt financing:
$$R_E = R_U + (R_U - R_D) \times (D/E) \times (1 - T_C)$$

Case III

- Now we add bankruptcy costs
- As the D/E ratio increases, the probability of bankruptcy increases
- This increased probability will increase the expected bankruptcy costs
- At some point, the additional value of the interest tax shield will be offset by the expected bankruptcy cost
- At this point, the value of the firm will start to decrease and the WACC will start to increase as more debt is added

17.29 Bankruptcy Costs

- Direct costs
  - Legal and administrative costs
  - Ultimately cause bondholders to incur additional losses
  - Disincentive to debt financing
- Financial distress
  - Significant problems in meeting debt obligations
  - Most firms that experience financial distress do not ultimately file for bankruptcy

17.30 More Bankruptcy Costs

- Indirect bankruptcy costs
  - Larger than direct costs, but more difficult to measure and estimate
  - Stockholders wish to avoid a formal bankruptcy filing
  - Bondholders want to keep existing assets intact so they can at least receive that money
  - Assets lose value as management spends time worrying about avoiding bankruptcy instead of running the business
  - Also have lost sales, interrupted operations and loss of valuable employees

17.31 Figure 17.6

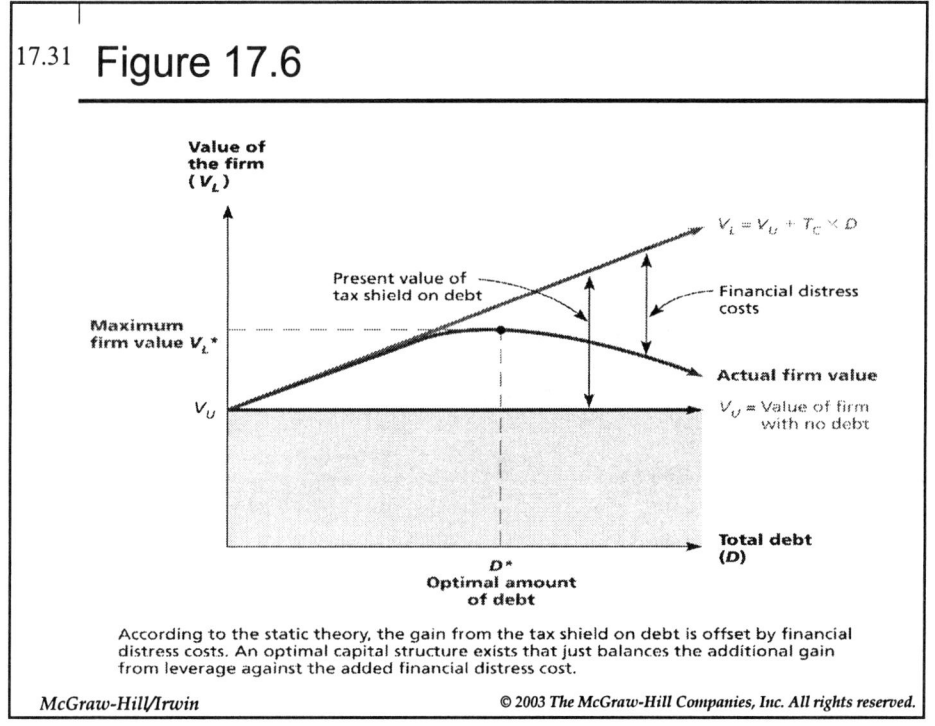

According to the static theory, the gain from the tax shield on debt is offset by financial distress costs. An optimal capital structure exists that just balances the additional gain from leverage against the added financial distress cost.

17.32 Figure 17.7

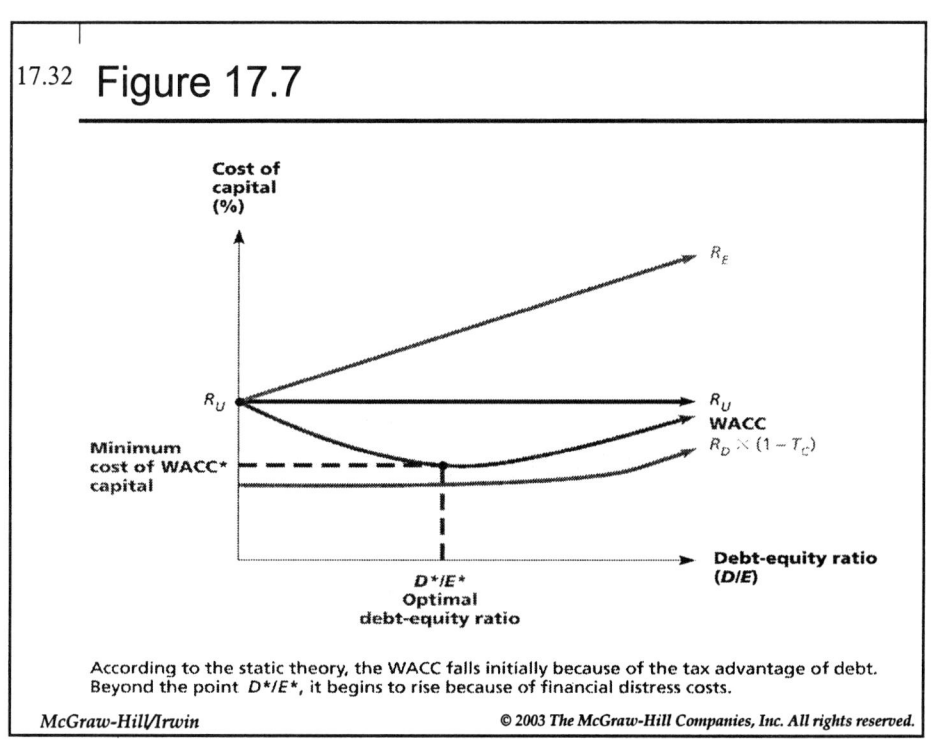

According to the static theory, the WACC falls initially because of the tax advantage of debt. Beyond the point D^*/E^*, it begins to rise because of financial distress costs.

17.33 Conclusions

- Case I – no taxes or bankruptcy costs
  - No optimal capital structure
- Case II – corporate taxes but no bankruptcy costs
  - Optimal capital structure is 100% debt
  - Each additional dollar of debt increases the cash flow of the firm
- Case III – corporate taxes and bankruptcy costs
  - Optimal capital structure is part debt and part equity
  - Occurs where the benefit from an additional dollar of debt is just offset by the increase in expected bankruptcy costs

17.34 Figure 17.8

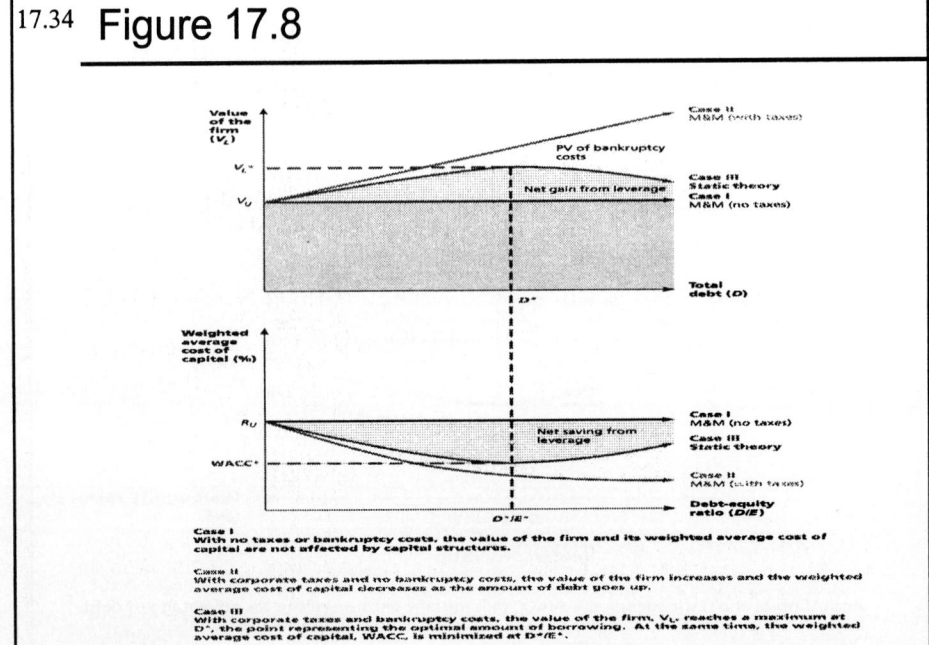

Managerial Recommendations

- The tax benefit is only important if the firm has a large tax liability
- Risk of financial distress
  - The greater the risk of financial distress, the less debt will be optimal for the firm
  - The cost of financial distress varies across firms and industries and as a manager you need to understand the cost for your industry

Figure 17.9

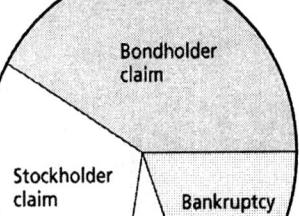

In the extended pie model, the value of all the claims against the firm's cash flows is not affected by capital structure, but the *relative* values of claims change as the amount of debt financing is increased.

17.37 The Value of the Firm

- Value of the firm = marketed claims + nonmarketed claims
  - Marketed claims are the claims of stockholders and bondholders
  - Nonmarketed claims are the claims of the government and other potential stakeholders
- The overall value of the firm is unaffected by changes in capital structure
- The division of value between marketed claims and nonmarketed claims may be impacted by capital structure decisions

17.38 Observed Capital Structure

- Capital structure does differ by industries
- Differences according to *Cost of Capital 2000 Yearbook by Ibbotson Associates, Inc.*
  - Lowest levels of debt
    - Drugs with 2.75% debt
    - Computers with 6.91% debt
  - Highest levels of debt
    - Steel with 55.84% debt
    - Department stores with 50.53% debt

17.39 Work the Web Example

- You can find information about a company's capital structure relative to its industry, sector and the S&P 500 at Yahoo Marketguide
- Click on the web surfer to go to the site
  - Choose a company and get a quote
  - Choose ratio comparisons

17.40 Bankruptcy Process – Part I

- Business failure – business has terminated with a loss to creditors
- Legal bankruptcy – petition federal court for bankruptcy
- Technical insolvency – firm is unable to meet debt obligations
- Accounting insolvency – book value of equity is negative

17.41 Bankruptcy Process – Part II

- Liquidation
  - Chapter 7 of the Federal Bankruptcy Reform Act of 1978
  - Trustee takes over assets, sells them and distributes the proceeds according to the absolute priority rule
- Reorganization
  - Chapter 11 of the Federal Bankruptcy Reform Act of 1978
  - Restructure the corporation with a provision to repay creditors

17.42 Quick Quiz

- Explain the effect of leverage on EPS and ROE
- What is the break-even EBIT?
- How do we determine the optimal capital structure?
- What is the optimal capital structure in the three cases that were discussed in this chapter?
- What is the difference between liquidation and reorganization?

18.1 Key Concepts and Skills

- Understand dividend types and how they are paid
- Understand the issues surrounding dividend policy decisions
- Understand the difference between cash and stock dividends
- Understand why share repurchases are an alternative to dividends

18.2 Chapter Outline

- Cash Dividends and Dividend Payment
- Does Dividend Policy Matter?
- Some Real-World Factors Favoring a Low Payout
- Some Real-World Factors Favoring a High Payout
- A Resolution of Real-World Factors
- Establishing a Dividend Policy
- Stock Repurchase: An Alternative to Cash Dividends
- Stock Dividends and Stock Splits

18.3 Cash Dividends

- Regular cash dividend – cash payments made directly to stockholders, usually each quarter
- Extra cash dividend – indication that the "extra" amount may not be repeated in the future
- Special cash dividend – similar to extra dividend, but definitely won't be repeated
- Liquidating dividend – some or all of the business has been sold

18.4 Dividend Payment

- Declaration Date – Board declares the dividend and it becomes a liability of the firm
- Ex-dividend Date
  - Occurs two business days before date of record
  - If you buy stock on or after this date, you will not receive the dividend
  - Stock price generally drops by about the amount of the dividend
- Date of Record – Holders of record are determined and they will receive the dividend payment
- Date of Payment – checks are mailed

Figure 18.2

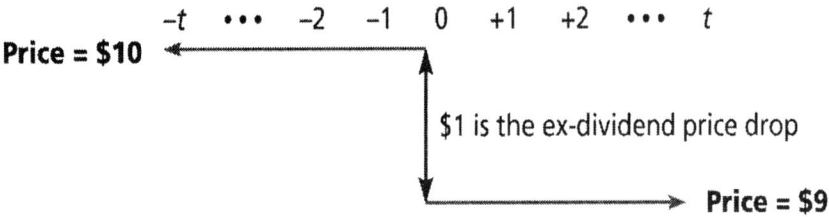

The stock price will fall by the amount of the dividend on the ex date (Time 0). If the dividend is $1 per share, the price will be $10 − 1 = $9 on the ex date:

    Before ex date (Time −1), dividend = $0   Price = $10
    On ex date (Time 0), dividend = $1   Price = $9

Does Dividend Policy Matter?

- Dividends matter – the value of the stock is based on the present value of expected future dividends
- Dividend policy may not matter
  - Dividend policy is the decision to pay dividends versus retaining funds to reinvest in the firm
  - In theory, if the firm reinvests capital now, it will grow and can pay higher dividends in the future

18.7 Illustration of Irrelevance

- Consider a firm that can either pay out dividends of $10,000 per year for each of the next two years or can pay $9000 this year, reinvest the other $1000 into the firm and then pay $11,120 next year. Investors require a 12% return.
  - Market Value with constant dividend = $16,900.51
  - Market Value with reinvestment = $16,900.51
- If the company will earn the required return, then it doesn't matter when it pays the dividends

18.8 Low Payout Please

- Why might a low payout be desirable?
- Individuals in upper income tax brackets might prefer lower dividend payouts, with the immediate tax consequences, in favor of higher capital gains
- Flotation costs – low payouts can decrease the amount of capital that needs to be raised, thereby lowering flotation costs
- Dividend restrictions – debt contracts might limit the percentage of income that can be paid out as dividends

18.9 High Payout Please

- Why might a high payout be desirable?
- Desire for current income
  - Individuals in low tax brackets
  - Groups that are prohibited from spending principal (trusts and endowments)
- Uncertainty resolution – no guarantee that the higher future dividends will materialize
- Taxes
  - Dividend exclusion for corporations
  - Tax-exempt investors don't have to worry about differential treatment between dividends and capital gains

18.10 Dividends and Signals

- Asymmetric information – managers have more information about the health of the company than investors
- Changes in dividends convey information
  - Dividend increases
    - Management believes it can be sustained
    - Expectation of higher future dividends, increasing present value
    - Signal of a healthy, growing firm
  - Dividend decreases
  - Management believes it can no longer sustain the current level of dividends
  - Expectation of lower dividends indefinitely; decreasing present value
  - Signal of a firm that is having financial difficulties

18.11 Clientele Effect

- Some investors prefer low dividend payouts and will buy stock in those companies that offer low dividend payouts
- Some investors prefer high dividend payouts and will buy stock in those companies that offer high dividend payouts

18.12 Implications of the Clientele Effect

- What do you think will happen if a firm changes its policy from a high payout to a low payout?
- What do you think will happen if a firm changes its policy from a low payout to a high payout?
- If this is the case, does dividend POLICY matter?

18.13 Dividend Policy in Practice

- Residual dividend policy
- Constant growth dividend policy – dividends increased at a constant rate each year
- Constant payout ratio – pay a constant percent of earnings each year
- Compromise dividend policy

18.14 Residual Dividend Policy

- Determine capital budget
- Determine target capital structure
- Finance investments with a combination of debt and equity in line with the target capital structure
  - Remember that retained earnings are equity
  - If additional equity is needed, issue new shares
- If there are excess earnings, then pay the remainder out in dividends

18.15 Example – Residual Dividend Policy

- Given
  - Need $5 million for new investments
  - Target capital structure: D/E = 2/3
  - Net Income = $4 million
- Finding dividend
  - 40% financed with debt (2 million)
  - 60% financed with equity (3 million)
  - NI – equity financing = $1 million, paid out as dividends

18.16 Compromise Dividend Policy

- Goals, ranked in order of importance
  - Avoid cutting back on positive NPV projects to pay a dividend
  - Avoid dividend cuts
  - Avoid the need to sell equity
  - Maintain a target debt/equity ratio
  - Maintain a target dividend payout ratio
- Companies want to accept positive NPV projects, while avoiding negative signals

18.17 Stock Repurchase

- Company buys back its own shares of stock
  - Tender offer – company states a purchase price and a desired number of shares
  - Open market – buys stock in the open market
- Similar to a cash dividend in that it returns cash from the firm to the stockholders
- This is another argument for dividend policy irrelevance in the absence of taxes or other imperfections

18.18 Real-World Considerations

- Stock repurchase allows investors to decide if they want the current cash flow and associated tax consequences
- Investors face capital gains taxes instead of ordinary income taxes (lower rate)
- In our current tax structure, repurchases may be more desirable due to the options provided stockholders
- The IRS recognizes this and will not allow a stock repurchase for the sole purpose of allowing investors to avoid taxes

18.19 Information Content of Stock Repurchases

- Stock repurchases sends a positive signal that management believes that the current price is low
- Tender offers send a more positive signal than open market repurchases because the company is stating a specific price
- The stock price often increases when repurchases are announced

18.20 Example: Repurchase Announcement

"America West Airlines announced that its Board of Directors has authorized the purchase of up to 2.5 million shares of its Class B common stock on the open market as circumstances warrant over the next two years …

"Following the approval of the stock repurchase program by the company's Board of Directors earlier today. W. A. Franke, chairman and chief officer said 'The stock repurchase program reflects our belief that America West stock may be an attractive investment opportunity for the Company, and it underscores our commitment to enhancing long-term shareholder value.'

"The shares will be repurchased with cash on hand, but only if and to the extent the Company holds unrestricted cash in excess of $200 million to ensure that an adequate level of cash and cash equivalents is maintained."

Stock Dividends

- Pay additional shares of stock instead of cash
- Increases the number of outstanding shares
- Small stock dividend
  - Less than 20 to 25%
  - If you own 100 shares and the company declared a 10% stock dividend, you would receive an additional 10 shares
- Large stock dividend – more than 20 to 25%

Stock Splits

- Stock splits – essentially the same as a stock dividend except expressed as a ratio
  - For example, a 2 for 1 stock split is the same as a 100% stock dividend
- Stock price is reduced when the stock splits
- Common explanation for split is to return price to a "more desirable trading range"

18.23 Quick Quiz

- What are the different types of dividends and how is a dividend paid?
- What is the clientele effect and how does it affect dividend policy relevance?
- What is the information content of dividend changes?
- What is the difference between a residual dividend policy and a compromise dividend policy?
- What are stock dividends and how do they differ from cash dividends?
- How are share repurchases an alternative to dividends and why might investors prefer them?

19.1 Key Concepts and Skills

- Understand the components of the cash cycle and why it is important
- Understand the pros and cons of the various short-term financing policies
- Be able to prepare a cash budget
- Understand the various options for short-term financing

19.2 Chapter Outline

- Tracing Cash and Net Working Capital
- The Operating Cycle and the Cash Cycle
- Some Aspects of Short-Term Financial Policy
- The Cash Budget
- Short-Term Borrowing
- A Short-Term Financial Plan

19.3 Sources and Uses of Cash

- Balance sheet identity (rearranged)
  - Net working capital + fixed assets = long-term debt + equity
  - Net working capital = cash + other CA – CL
  - Cash = long-term debt + equity + current liabilities – current assets other than cash – fixed assets
- Sources
  - Increasing long-term debt, equity or current liabilities
  - Decreasing current assets other than cash or fixed assets
- Uses
  - Decreasing long-term debt, equity or current liabilities
  - Increasing current assets other than cash or fixed assets

19.4 The Operating Cycle

- Operating cycle – time between purchasing the inventory and collecting the cash
- Inventory period – time required to purchase and sell the inventory
- Accounts receivable period – time to collect on credit sales
- Operating cycle = inventory period + accounts receivable period

19.5 Cash Cycle

- Cash cycle
  - time period for which we need to finance our inventory
  - Difference between when we receive cash from the sale and when we have to pay for the inventory
- Accounts payable period – time between purchase of inventory and payment for the inventory
- Cash cycle = Operating cycle – accounts payable period

19.6 Figure 19.1

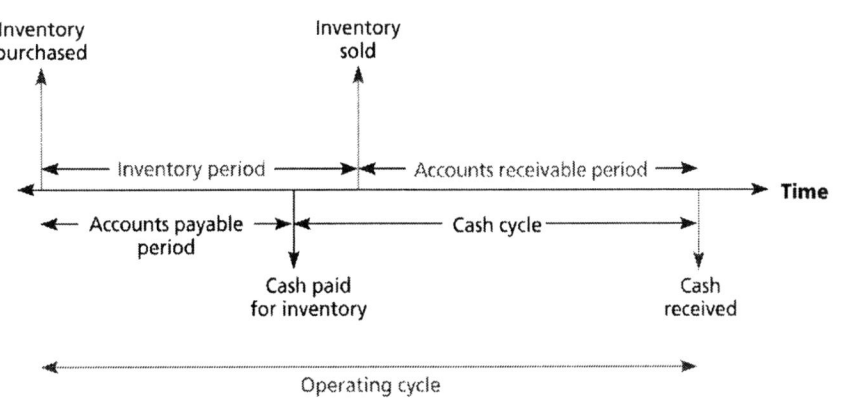

The operating cycle is the time period from inventory purchase until the receipt of cash. (The operating cycle may not include the time from placement of the order until arrival of the stock.) The cash cycle is the time period from when cash is paid out to when cash is received.

19.7 Example Information

- Inventory:
  - Beginning = 5000
  - Ending = 6000
- Accounts Receivable:
  - Beginning = 4000
  - Ending = 5000
- Accounts Payable:
  - Beginning = 2200
  - Ending = 3500
- Net sales = 30,000
- Cost of Goods sold = 12,000

19.8 Example – Operating Cycle

- Inventory period
  - Average inventory = (5000 + 6000)/2 = 5500
  - Inventory turnover = 12,000 / 5500 = 2.18 times
  - Inventory period = 365 / 2.18 = 167 days
- Receivables period
  - Average receivables = (4000 + 5000)/2 = 4500
  - Receivables turnover = 30,000/4500 = 6.67 times
  - Receivables period = 365 / 6.67 = 55 days
- Operating cycle = 167 + 55 = 222 days

19.9 Example – Cash Cycle

- Payables Period
  - Average payables = (2200 + 3500)/2 = 2850
  - Payables turnover = 12,000/2850 = 4.21
  - Payables period = 365 / 4.21 = 87 days
- Cash Cycle = 222 – 87 = 135 days
- We have to finance our inventory for 135 days
- We need to be looking more carefully at our receivables and our payables periods – they both seem extensive

19.10 Short-Term Financial Policy

- Size of investments in current assets
  - Flexible policy – maintain a high ratio of current assets to sales
  - Restrictive policy – maintain a low ratio of current assets to sales
- Financing of current assets
  - Flexible policy – less short-term debt and more long-term debt
  - Restrictive policy – more short-term debt and less long-term debt

19.11 Carrying vs. Shortage Costs

- Managing short-term assets involves a trade-off between carrying costs and shortage costs
  - Carrying costs – increase with increased levels of current assets, the costs to store and finance the assets
  - Shortage costs – decrease with increased levels of current assets, the costs to replenish assets
    - Trading or order costs
    - Costs related to safety reserves, i.e., lost sales and customers and production stoppages

19.12 Temporary vs. Permanent Assets

- Temporary current assets
  - Sales or required inventory build-up are often seasonal
  - The additional current assets carried during the "peak" time
  - The level of current assets will decrease as sales occur
- Permanent current assets
  - Firms generally need to carry a minimum level of current assets at all times
  - These assets are considered "permanent" because the level is constant, not because the assets aren't sold

Figure 19.4

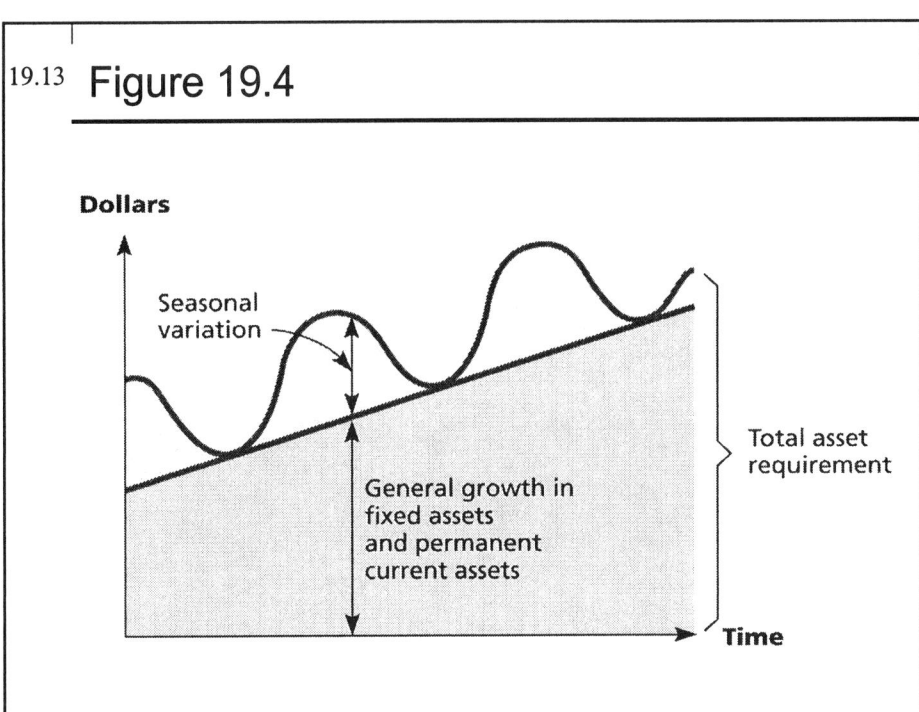

Choosing the Best Policy

- Cash reserves
  - Pros – firms will be less likely to experience financial distress and are better able to handle emergencies or take advantage of unexpected opportunities
  - Cons – cash and marketable securities earn a lower return and are zero NPV investments
- Maturity hedging
  - Try to match financing maturities with asset maturities
  - Finance temporary current assets with short-term debt
  - Finance permanent current assets and fixed assets with long-term debt and equity
- Interest Rates
  - Short-term rates are normally lower than long-term rates, so it may be cheaper to finance with short-term debt
  - Firms can get into trouble if rates increase quickly or if it begins to have difficulty making payments – may not be able to refinance the short-term loans
- Have to consider all these factors and determine a compromise policy that fits the needs of your firm

Figure 19.6

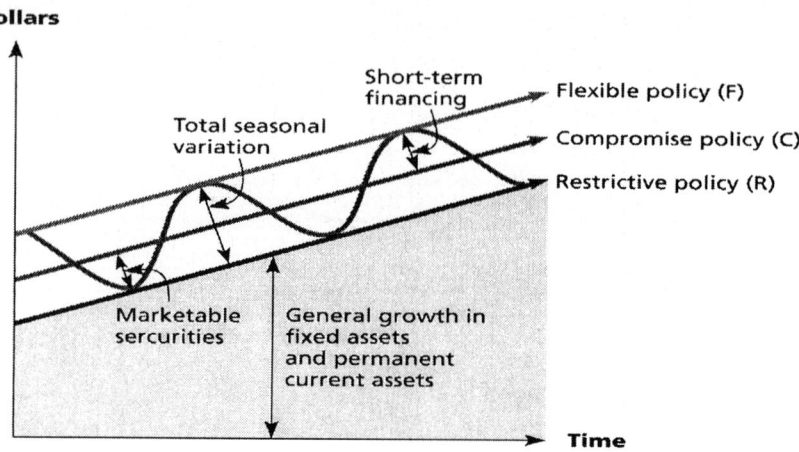

With a compromise policy, the firm keeps a reserve of liquidity that it uses to initially finance seasonal variations in current asset needs. Short-term borrowing is used when the reserve is exhausted.

Cash Budget

- Forecast of cash inflows and outflows over the next short-term planning period
- Primary tool in short-term financial planning
- Helps determine when the firm should experience cash surpluses and when it will need to borrow to cover working-capital costs
- Allows a company to plan ahead and begin the search for financing before the money is actually needed

19.17 Example: Cash Budget Information

- Pet Treats Inc. specializes in gourmet pet treats and receives all income from sales
- Sales estimates (in millions)
  - Q1 = 500; Q2 = 600; Q3 = 650; Q4 = 800; Q1 next year = 550
- Accounts receivable
  - Beginning receivables = $250
  - Average collection period = 30 days
- Accounts payable
  - Purchases = 50% of next quarter's sales
  - Beginning payables = 125
  - Accounts payable period is 45 days
- Other expenses
  - Wages, taxes and other expense are 25% of sales
  - Interest and dividend payments are $50
  - A major capital expenditure of $200 is expected in the second quarter
- The initial cash balance is $100 and the company maintains a minimum balance of $50

19.18 Example: Cash Budget – Cash Collections

- ACP = 30 days, this implies that 2/3 of sales are collected in the quarter made and the remaining 1/3 are collected the following quarter
- Beginning receivables of $250 will be collected in the first quarter

	Q1	Q2	Q3	Q4
Beginning Receivables	250	167	200	217
Sales	500	600	650	800
Cash Collections	583	567	633	750
Ending Receivables	167	200	217	267

Example: Cash Budget – Cash Disbursements

- Payables period is 45 days, so half of the purchases will be paid for each quarter and the remaining will be paid the following quarter
- Beginning payables = $125

	Q1	Q2	Q3	Q4
Payment of accounts	275	438	362	338
Wages, taxes and other expenses	125	150	163	200
Capital expenditures		200		
Interest and dividend payments	50	50	50	50
Total cash disbursements	450	838	575	588

Example: Cash Budget – Net Cash Flow and Cash Balance

	Q1	Q2	Q3	Q4
Total cash collections	583	567	633	750
Total cash disbursements	450	838	575	588
Net cash inflow	133	-271	58	162
Beginning Cash Balance	100	233	-38	20
Net cash inflow	133	-271	58	162
Ending cash balance	233	-38	20	182
Minimum cash balance	-50	-50	-50	-50
Cumulative surplus (deficit)	183	-88	-30	132

19.21 Short-Term Borrowing

- Unsecured Loans
  - Line of credit
  - Committed vs. noncommitted
  - Revolving credit arrangement
  - Letter of credit
- Secured Loans
  - Accounts receivable financing
    - Assigning
    - Factoring
  - Inventory loans
    - Blanket inventory lien
    - Trust receipt
    - Field warehouse financing
- Commercial Paper
- Trade Credit

19.22 Example: Compensating Balance

- We have a $500,000 line of credit with a 15% compensating balance requirement. The quoted interest rate is 9%. We need to borrow $150,000 for inventory for one year.
  - How much do we need to borrow?
    - $150,000/(1-.15) = 176,471$
  - What interest rate are we effectively paying?
    - Interest paid = $176,471(.09) = 15,882$
    - Effective rate = $15,882/150,000 = .1059$ or 10.59%

Example: Factoring

- Last year your company had average accounts receivable of $2 million. Credit sales were $24 million. You factor receivables by discounting them 2%. What is the effective rate of interest?
  - Receivables turnover = 24/2 = 12 times
  - Average collection period = 365/12 = 30.4 days
  - APR = 12(.02/.98) = .2449 or 24.49%
  - EAR = $(1+.02/.98)^{12} - 1$ = .2743 or 27.43%

Short-Term Financial Plan

	Q1	Q2	Q3	Q4
Beginning cash balance	100	233	50	50
Net cash inflow	133	-271	58	162
New short-term borrowing		88		
Interest on short-term borrowing			3	1
Short-term borrowing repaid			55	33
Ending cash balance	233	50	50	178
Minimum cash balance	-50	-50	-50	-50
Cumulative surplus (deficit)	183	0	0	128
Beginning short-term debt	0		88	33
Change in short-term debt	0	88	-55	-33
Ending short-term debt	0	88	33	0

Quick Quiz

- How do you compute the operating cycle and the cash cycle?
- What are the differences between a flexible short-term financing policy and a restrictive one? What are the pros and cons of each?
- What are the key components of a cash budget?
- What are the major forms of short-term borrowing?

20.1 Key Concepts and Skills

- Understand how firms manage cash
- Understand float
- Understand how to accelerate collections and manage disbursements
- Understand the characteristics of various short-term securities
- Appendix: Be able to use the BAT and Miller-Orr models and understand the different assumptions

20.2 Chapter Outline

- Reasons for Holding Cash
- Understanding Float
- Cash Collection and Concentration
- Managing Cash Disbursements
- Investing Idle Cash
- Appendix
  - The Basic Idea
  - The BAT Model
  - The Miller-Orr Model: A More General Approach
  - Implications of the BAT and Miller-Orr Models
  - Other Factors Influencing the Target Cash Balance

20.3 Reasons for Holding Cash

- Speculative motive – hold cash to take advantage of unexpected opportunities
- Precautionary motive – hold cash in case of emergencies
- Transaction motive – hold cash to pay the day-to-day bills
- Trade-off between opportunity cost of holding cash relative to the transaction cost of converting marketable securities to cash for transactions

20.4 Understanding Float

- Float – difference between cash balance recorded in the cash account and the cash balance recorded at the bank
- Disbursement float
  - Generated when a firm writes checks
  - Available balance at bank – book balance > 0
- Collection float
  - Checks received increase book balance before the bank credits the account
  - Available balance at bank – book balance < 0
- Net float = disbursement float + collection float

20.5 Example: Types of Float

- You have $3000 in your checking account. You just deposited $2000 and wrote a check for $2500.
    - What is the disbursement float?
    - What is the collection float?
    - What is the net float?
    - What is your book balance?
    - What is your available balance?

20.6 Example: Measuring Float

- Size of float depends on the dollar amount and the time delay
- Delay = mailing time + processing delay + availability delay
- Suppose you mail a check for $1000 and it takes 3 days to reach its destination, 1 day to process and 1 day before the bank will make the cash available
- What is the average daily float (assuming 30 day months)?
    - Method 1: (3+1+1)(1000)/30 = 166.67
    - Method 2: (5/30)(1000) + (25/30)(0) = 166.67

20.7 Example: Cost of Float

- Cost of float – opportunity cost of not being able to use the money
- Suppose the average daily float is $3 million with a weighted average delay of 5 days.
  - What is the total amount unavailable to earn interest?
    - 5*3 million = 15 million
  - What is the NPV of a project that could reduce the delay by 3 days if the cost is $8 million?
    - Immediate cash inflow = 3*3 million = 9 million
    - NPV = 9 – 8 = $1 million

20.8 Cash Collection

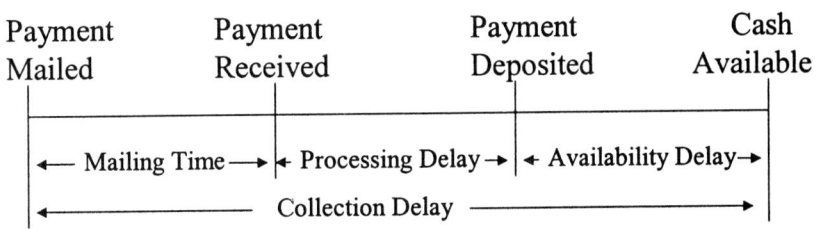

One of the goals of float management is to try and reduce the collection delay. There are several techniques that can reduce various parts of the delay.

20.9 Example: Accelerating Collections – Part I

- Your company does business nationally and currently all checks are sent to the headquarters in Tampa, FL. You are considering a lock-box system that will have checks processed in Phoenix, St. Louis and Philadelphia. The Tampa office will continue to process the checks it receives in house.
  - Collection time will be reduced by 2 days on average
  - Daily interest rate on T-billls = .01%
  - Average number of daily payments to each lockbox is 5000
  - Average size of payment is $500
  - The processing fee is $.10 per check plus $10 to wire funds to a centralized bank at the end of each day.

20.10 Example: Accelerating Collections – Part II

- Benefits
  - Average daily collections = 3(5000)(500) = 7,500,000
  - Increased bank balance = 2(7,500,000) = 15,000,000
- Costs
  - Daily cost = .1(15,000) + 3*10 = 1530
  - Present value of daily cost = 1530/.0001 = 15,300,000
- NPV = 15,000,000 – 15,300,000 = -300,000
- The company should not accept this lock-box proposal

Cash Disbursements

- Slowing down payments can increase disbursement float – but it may not be ethical or optimal to do this
- Controlling disbursements
  - Zero-balance account
  - Controlled disbursement account

Investing Cash

- Money market – financial instruments with an original maturity of one-year or less
- Temporary Cash Surpluses
  - Seasonal or cyclical activities – buy marketable securities with seasonal surpluses, convert securities back to cash when deficits occur
  - Planned or possible expenditures – accumulate marketable securities in anticipation of upcoming expenses

Figure 20.6

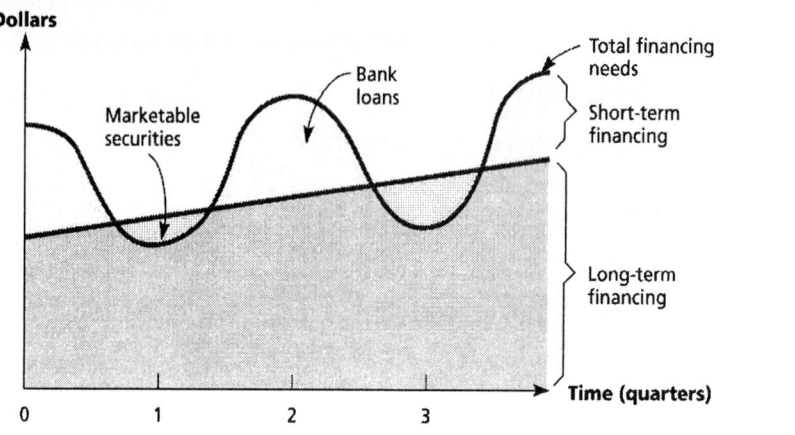

Time 1: A surplus cash flow exists. Seasonal demand for assets is low. The surplus cash flow is invested in short-term marketable securities.

Time 2: A deficit cash flow exists. Seasonal demand for assets is high. The financial deficit is financed by the selling of marketable securities and by bank borrowing.

Characteristics of Short-Term Securities

- Maturity – firms often limit the maturity of short-term investments to 90 days to avoid loss of principal due to changing interest rates
- Default risk – avoid investing in marketable securities with significant default risk
- Marketability – ease of converting to cash
- Taxability – consider different tax characteristics when making a decision

Quick Quiz

- What are the major reasons for holding cash?
- What is the difference between disbursement float and collection float?
- How does a lock box system work?
- What are the major characteristics of short-term securities?

20A.1 Target Cash Balances

- Target cash balance – desired cash level determined by trade-off between carrying costs and shortage costs
- Flexible policy - If a firm maintains a marketable securities account, the primary shortage cost is the trading cost from buying and selling securities
- Restrictive policy – Generally borrow short-term, so the shortage costs will be the fees and interest associated with arranging a loan

20A.2 Figure 20A.1

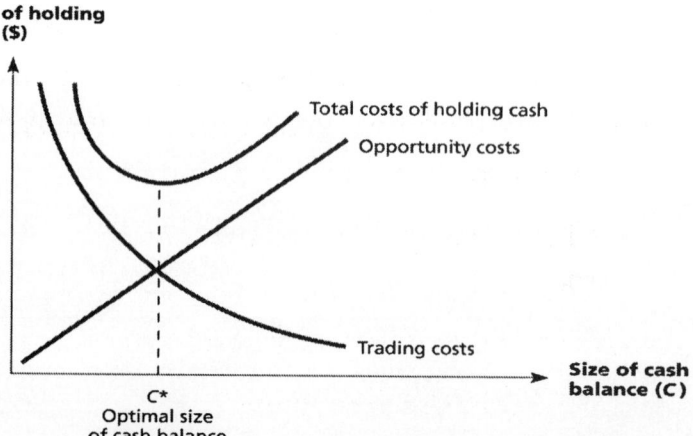

Trading costs are increased when the firm must sell securities to establish a cash balance. Opportunity costs are increased when there is a cash balance because there is no return on cash.

20A.3 BAT Model

- Assumptions
  - Cash is spent at the same rate every day
  - Cash expenditures are known with certainty
- Optimal cash balance is where opportunity cost of holding cash = trading cost
  - Opportunity cost = (C/2)*R
  - Trading cost = (T/C)*F
  - Total cost = (C/2)*R + (T/C)*F

$$C^* = \sqrt{\frac{2TF}{R}}$$

20A.4 Example: BAT Model

- Your firm will have $5 million in cash expenditures over the next year. The interest rate is 4% and the fixed trading cost is $25 per transaction.
  - What is the optimal cash balance?
  - What is the average cash balance?
  - What is the opportunity cost?
  - What is the shortage cost?
  - What is the total cost?

20A.5 Miller-Orr Model

- Model for cash inflows and outflows that fluctuate randomly
- Define an upper limit, a lower limit and a target balance
  - Management sets lower limit, L
  - $C^* = L + [(3/4)F\sigma^2/R]^{1/3}$ (target balance)
  - $U^* = 3C^* - 2L$ (upper limit)
  - Average cash balance = $(4C^* - L)/3$

20A.6 Figure 20A.3

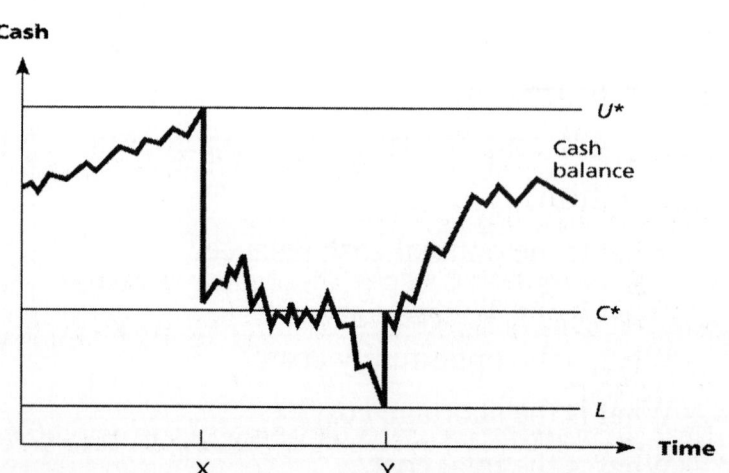

U^* is the upper control limit. L is the lower control limit. The target cash balance is C^*. As long as cash is between L and U^*, no transaction is made.

20A.7 Example: Miller-Orr Model

- Suppose that we wish to maintain a minimum cash balance of $50,000. Our fixed trading cost is $250 per trade, the interest rate is .5% per month and the standard deviation of monthly cash flows is $10,000.
  - What is the target cash balance?
  - What is the upper limit?
  - What is the average cash balance?

20A.8 Conclusions

- The greater the interest rate, the lower the target cash balance
- The greater the fixed order cost, the higher the target cash balance
- It is generally more expensive to borrow needed funds than it is to sell marketable securities
- Trading costs are usually very small relative to opportunity costs for large firms

21.1 Key Concepts

- Understand the key issues related to credit management
- Understand the impact of cash discounts
- Be able to evaluate a proposed credit policy
- Understand the components of credit analysis
- Understand the major components of inventory management
- Be able to use the EOQ model to determine optimal inventory levels

21.2 Chapter Outline

- Credit and Receivables
- Terms of the Sale
- Analyzing Credit Policy
- Optimal Credit Policy
- Credit Analysis
- Collection Policy
- Inventory Management
- Inventory Management Techniques
- Appendix
  - Two Alternative Approaches
  - Discounts and Default Risk

21.3 Credit Management: Key Issues

- Granting credit increases sales
- Costs of granting credit
  - Chance that customers won't pay
  - Financing receivables
- Credit management examines the trade-off between increased sales and the costs of granting credit

21.4 Components of Credit Policy

- Terms of sale
  - Credit period
  - Cash discount and discount period
  - Type of credit instrument
- Credit analysis – distinguishing between "good" customers that will pay and "bad" customers that will default
- Collection policy – effort expended on collecting on receivables

21.5 The Cash Flows from Granting Credit

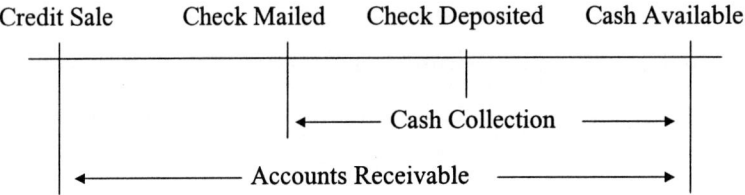

21.6 Terms of Sale

- Basic Form: 2/10 net 45
    - 2% discount if paid in 10 days
    - Total amount due in 45 days if discount not taken
- Buy $500 worth of merchandise with the credit terms given above
    - Pay $500(1 - .02) = $490 if you pay in 10 days
    - Pay $500 if you pay in 45 days

21.7 Example: Cash Discounts

- Finding the implied interest rate when customers do not take the discount
- Credit terms of 2/10 net 45 and $500 loan
  - $10 interest (.02*500)
  - Period rate = 10 / 490 = 2.0408%
  - Period = (45 − 10) = 35 days
  - 365 / 35 = 10.4286 periods per year
- EAR = $(1.020408)^{10.4286} - 1 = 23.45\%$
- The company benefits when customers choose to forego discounts

21.8 Credit Policy Effects

- Revenue Effects
  - Delay in receiving cash from sale
  - May be able to increase price
  - May increase total sales
- Cost Effects
  - Cost of sale is still incurred even though the cash from the sale has not been received
  - Cost of debt – must finance receivables
  - Probability of nonpayment – some percentage customers will not pay for products purchased
  - Cash discount – some customers will pay early and pay less than the full sales price

21.9 Example: Evaluating a Proposed Policy – Part I

- Your company is evaluating a switch from a cash only policy to a net 30 policy. The price per unit is $100 and the variable cost per unit is $40. The company currently sells 1000 units per month. Under the proposed policy the company will sell 1050 units per month. The required monthly return is 1.5%.
- What is the NPV of the switch?
- Should the company offer credit terms of net 30?

21.10 Example: Evaluating a Proposed Policy – Part II

- Incremental cash inflow
  - $(100 - 40)(1050 - 1000) = 3000$
- Present value of incremental cash inflow
  - $3000/.015 = 200,000$
- Cost of switching
  - $100(1000) + 40(1050 - 1000) = 102,000$
- NPV of switching
  - $200,000 - 102,000 = 98,000$
- Yes the company should switch

21.11 Total Cost of Granting Credit

- Carrying costs
  - Required return on receivables
  - Losses from bad debts
  - Costs of managing credit and collections
- Shortage costs
  - Lost sales due to a restrictive credit policy
- Total cost curve
  - Sum of carrying costs and shortage costs
  - Optimal credit policy is where the total cost curve is minimized

21.12 Credit Analysis

- Process of deciding which customers receive credit
- Gathering information
  - Financial statements
  - Credit reports
  - Banks
  - Payment history with the firm
- Determining Creditworthiness
  - 5 Cs of Credit
  - Credit Scoring

21.13 Example: One Time Sale

- NPV = -v + (1 - π)P / (1 + R)
- Your company is considering granting credit to a new customer. The variable cost per unit is $50, the current price is $110, the probability of default is 15% and the monthly required return is 1%.
- NPV = -50 + (1-.15)(110)/(1.01) = 42.57
- What is the break-even probability?
  - 0 = -50 + (1 - π)(110)/(1.01)
  - π = .5409 or 54.09%

21.14 Example: Repeat Customers

- NPV = -v + (1-π)(P – v)/R
- Look at the previous example, what is the NPV if we are looking at repeat business?
- NPV = -50 + (1-.15)(110 – 50)/.01 = 5,050
- Repeat customers can be very valuable (hence the importance of good customer service)
- It may make sense to grant credit to almost everyone once, as long as the variable cost is low relative to the price
- If a customer defaults once, you don't grant credit again

Credit Information

- Financial statements
- Credit reports with customer's payment history to other firms
- Banks
- Payment history with the company

Five Cs of Credit

- Character – willingness to meet financial obligations
- Capacity – ability to meet financial obligations out of operating cash flows
- Capital – financial reserves
- Collateral – assets pledged as security
- Conditions – general economic conditions related to customer's business

21.17 Collection Policy

- Monitoring receivables
  - Keep an eye on average collection period relative to your credit terms
  - Use an aging schedule to determine percentage of payments that are being made late
- Collection policy
  - Delinquency letter
  - Telephone call
  - Collection agency
  - Legal action

21.18 Inventory Management

- Inventory can be a large percentage of a firm's assets
- Costs associated with carrying too much inventory
- Costs associated with not carrying enough inventory
- Inventory management tries to find the optimal trade-off between carrying too much inventory versus not enough

21.19 Types of Inventory

- Manufacturing firm
  - Raw material – starting point in production process
  - Work-in-progress
  - Finished goods – products ready to ship or sell
- Remember that one firm's "raw material" may be another company's "finished good"
- Different types of inventory can vary dramatically in terms of liquidity

21.20 Inventory Costs

- Carrying costs – range from 20 – 40% of inventory value per year
  - Storage and tracking
  - Insurance and taxes
  - Losses due to obsolescence, deterioration or theft
  - Opportunity cost of capital
- Shortage costs
  - Restocking costs
  - Lost sales or lost customers
- Consider both types of costs and minimize the total cost

21.21 Inventory Management - ABC

- Classify inventory by cost, demand and need
- Those items that have substantial shortage costs should be maintained in larger quantities than those with lower shortage costs
- Generally maintain smaller quantities of expensive items
- Maintain a substantial supply of less expensive basic materials

21.22 EOQ Model

- The EOQ model minimizes the total inventory cost
- Total carrying cost = (average inventory) x (carrying cost per unit) = (Q/2)(CC)
- Total restocking cost = (fixed cost per order) x (number of orders) = F(T/Q)
- Total Cost = Total carrying cost + total restocking cost = (Q/2)(CC) + F(T/Q)

$$Q^* = \sqrt{\frac{2\,TF}{CC}}$$

Example: EOQ

- Consider an inventory item that has carrying cost = $1.50 per unit. The fixed order cost is $50 per order and the firm sells 100,000 units per year.
  - What is the economic order quantity?

$$Q^* = \sqrt{\frac{2(100,000)(50)}{1.50}} = 2582$$

Extensions

- Safety stocks
  - Minimum level of inventory kept on hand
  - Increases carrying costs
- Reorder points
  - At what inventory level should you place an order?
  - Need to account for delivery time
- Derived-Demand Inventories
  - Materials Requirements Planning (MRP)
  - Just-in-Time Inventory

Quick Quiz

- What are the key issues associated with credit management?
- What are the cash flows from granting credit?
- How would you analyze a change in credit policy?
- How would you analyze whether to grant credit to a new customer?
- What is ABC inventory management?
- How do you use the EOQ model to determine optimal inventory levels?

21A.1 Alternative Credit Policy Analysis

- One-Shot Approach
  - Determine if you would be better off with the cash (with lower sales) this month or the cash (with higher sales) next month
  - Find the NPV of the investment as a one shot deal
  - Then determine the PV if this is repeated each month indefinitely

- Accounts Receivable Approach
  - Incremental investment in receivables = $PQ + v(Q' - Q)$
  - Carrying cost = $[PQ + v(Q' - Q)]R$
  - Compute present value of monthly benefit

21A.2 Discounts and Default

- Cash discounts and default affect the benefits received
  - Net incremental cash flow = $P'Q(d - \pi)$
  - NPV = $-PQ + P'Q(d - \pi)/R$
- Break-even Point
  - $\pi = d - R(1 - d)$

22.1 Key Concepts and Skills

- Understand how exchange rates are quoted and what they mean
- Know the difference between spot and forward rates
- Understand purchasing power parity and interest rate parity and the implications for changes in exchange rates
- Understand the basics of international capital budgeting
- Understand the impact of political risk on international business investing

22.2 Chapter Outline

- Terminology
- Foreign Exchange Markets and Exchange Rates
- Purchasing Power Parity
- Interest Rate Parity, Unbiased Forward Rates, and the International Fisher Effect
- International Capital Budgeting
- Exchange Rate Risk
- Political Risk

22.3 Domestic Financial Management and International Financial Management

- Considerations in International Financial Management
  - Have to consider the effect of exchange rates when operating in more than one currency
  - Have to consider the political risk associated with actions of foreign governments
  - More financing opportunities when you consider the international capital markets and this may reduce the firm's cost of capital

22.4 International Finance Terminology

- American Depository Receipt (ADR)
- Cross-rate
- Eurobond
- Eurocurrency (Eurodollars)
- Foreign bonds
- Gilts
- London Interbank Offer Rate (LIBOR)
- Swaps

22.5 Global Capital Markets

- The number of exchanges in foreign countries continues to increase, as does the liquidity on those exchanges
- Exchanges that allow for the flow of capital are extremely important to developing countries
- The United States has one of the most developed capital markets in the world, but foreign markets are becoming more competitive and are often willing to try more innovative ways to do business

22.6 Work the Web Example

- Thinking about going to Mexico for spring break or Japan for your summer vacation?
- How many pesos or yen can you get in exchange for $1000?
- Click on the web surfer to find out

22.7 Exchange Rates

- The price of one country's currency in terms of another
- Most currency is quoted in terms of dollars
- Consider the following quote:
  - France (Franc)   .1460   6.8479
  - The first number (.1460) is how many U.S. dollars it takes to buy 1 French Franc
  - The second number (6.8479) is how many French Francs it takes to buy $1
  - The two numbers are reciprocals of each other (1/6.8479 = .1460)

22.8 Example: Exchange Rates

- Suppose you have $10,000. Based on the rates in Figure 18.1, how many Italian Lira can you buy?
  - Exchange rate = 2021.37 Lira per U.S. dollar
  - Buy 10,000(2021.37) = 20,213,700 Lira
- Suppose you are visiting London and you want to buy a souvenir that costs 1000 British pounds. How much does it cost in U.S. dollars?
  - Exchange rate = .6669 pounds per dollar
  - Cost = 1000 / .6669 = $1499.48

22.9 Example: Triangle Arbitrage

- We observe the following quotes
  - 10.00 FF per $1
  - 2.00 DM per $1
  - 4.00 FF per DM
- What is the cross rate?
  - (10.00 FF/$1) / (2.00 DM/$1) = 5 FF per DM
- We have $100 to invest; buy low, sell high
  - Buy $100(10 FF/$1) = 1000 FF, use FF to buy DM
  - Buy 1000FF / (4 FF/DM) = 250 DM, use DM to buy dollars
  - Buy 250 DM / (2 DM/$1) = $125
  - Make $25 risk-free

22.10 Types of Transactions

- Spot trade – exchange currency immediately
  - Spot rate – the exchange rate for an immediate trade
- Forward trade – agree today to exchange currency at some future date and some specified price (also called a forward contract)
  - Forward rate – the exchange rate specified in the forward contract
  - If the forward rate is higher than the spot rate, the foreign currency is selling at a premium (when quoted as $ equivalents)
  - If the forward rate is lower than the spot rate, the foreign currency is selling at a discount

22.11 Absolute Purchasing Power Parity

- Price of an item is the same regardless of the currency used to purchase it
- Requirements for absolute PPP to hold
  - Transaction costs are zero
  - No barriers to trade (no taxes, tariffs, etc.)
  - No difference in the commodity between locations
- Absolute PPP rarely holds in practice for many goods

22.12 Relative Purchasing Power Parity

- Provides information about what causes changes in exchange rates
- The basic result is that exchange rates depend on relative inflation between countries
- $E(S_t) = S_0[1 + (h_{FC} - h_{US})]^t$
- Because absolute PPP doesn't hold for many goods, we will focus on relative PPP from here on out

Example: PPP

- Suppose the Canadian spot exchange rate is 1.4680 Canadian dollars per U.S. dollar. U.S. inflation is expected to be 3% per year and Canadian inflation is expected to be 2%.
  - Do you expect the U.S. dollar to appreciate or depreciate relative to the Canadian dollar?
    - Since inflation is higher in the US, we would expect the US dollar to depreciate relative to the Canadian dollar.
  - What is the expected exchange in one year?
    - $E(S_1) = 1.4680[1 + (.02 - .03)]^1 = 1.4533$

Covered Interest Arbitrage

- Examine the relationship between spot rates, forward rates and nominal rates between countries
- Again, the formulas will assume that the exchange rates are quoted in terms of foreign currency per U.S. dollar
- The U.S. risk-free rate is assumed to be the T-bill rate

22.15 Example: Covered Interest Arbitrage

- Consider the following information
  - $S_0 = 2$ DM / \$ $R_{US} = 10\%$
  - $F_1 = 1.8$ DM / \$ $R_G = 5\%$
- What is the arbitrage opportunity?
  - Borrow \$100 at 10%
  - Buy \$100(2 DM/\$) = 200 DM and invest at 5% for 1 year
  - In 1 year, receive 200(1.05) = 210 DM and convert back to dollars
  - 210 DM / (1.8 DM / \$) = \$116.67 and repay loan
  - Profit = 116.67 − 100(1.1) = \$6.67 risk free

22.16 Interest Rate Parity

- Based on the previous example, there must be a forward rate that would prevent the arbitrage opportunity.
- Interest rate parity defines what that forward rate should be

$$\text{Exact} : \frac{F_1}{S_0} = \frac{(1 + R_{FC})}{(1 + R_{US})}$$

$$\text{Approx.} : \frac{F_1}{S_0} = 1 + (R_{FC} - R_{US})$$

22.17 Unbiased Forward Rates

- The current forward rate is an unbiased estimate of the future spot exchange rate
- This means that on average the forward rate will equal the future spot rate
  - If the forward rate is consistently too high
    - Those who want to exchange yen for dollars would only be willing to transact in the future spot market
    - The forward price would have to come down for trades to occur
  - If the forward rate is consistently too low
    - Those who want to exchange dollars for yen would only be willing to transact in the future spot market
    - The forward price would have to come up for trades to occur

22.18 Uncovered Interest Parity

- What we know so far
  - PPP: $E(S_1) = S_0[1 + (h_{FC} - h_{US})]$
  - IRP: $F_1 = S_0[1 + (R_{FC} - R_{US})]$
  - UFR: $F_1 = E(S_1)$
- Combining the formulas we get
  - $E(S_1) = S_0[1 + (R_{FC} - R_{US})]$ for one period
  - $E(S_t) = S_0[1 + (R_{FC} - R_{US})]^t$

22.19 International Fisher Effect

- Combining PPP and UIP we can get the International Fisher Effect
- $R_{US} - h_{US} = R_{FC} - h_{FC}$
- The International Fisher Effect tells us that the real rate of return must be constant across countries
- If it is not, investors will move their money to the country with the higher real rate of return

22.20 Overseas Production: Alternative Approaches

- Home Currency Approach
  - Estimate cash flows in foreign currency
  - Estimate future exchange rates using UIP
  - Convert future cash flows to dollars
  - Discount using domestic required return
- Foreign Currency Approach
  - Estimate cash flows in foreign currency
  - Use the IFE to convert domestic required return to foreign required return
  - Discount using foreign required return
  - Convert NPV to dollars using current spot rate

22.21 Home Currency Approach

- Your company is looking at a new project in Mexico. The project will cost 9 million pesos. The cash flows are expected to be 2.25 million pesos per year for 5 years. The current spot exchange rate is 9.08 pesos per dollar. The risk-free rate in the US is 4% and the risk-free rate in Mexico 8%. The dollar required return is 15%.
  - Should the company make the investment?

22.22 Foreign Currency Approach

- Use the same information as the previous example to estimate the NPV using the Foreign Currency Approach
  - Mexican inflation rate from the International Fisher Effect is 8% - 4% = 4%
  - Required Return = 15% + 4% = 19%
  - PV of future cash flows = 6,879,679
  - NPV = 6,879,679 − 9,000,000 = -2,120,321 pesos
  - NPV = -2,120,321 / 9.08 = -233,516

22.23 Repatriated Cash Flows

- Often some of the cash generated from a foreign project must remain in the foreign country due to restrictions on repatriation
- Repatriation can occur in several ways
  - Dividends to parent company
  - Management fees for central services
  - Royalties on the use of trade names and patents

22.24 Short-Run Exposure

- Risk from day-to-day fluctuations in exchange rates and the fact that companies have contracts to buy and sell goods in the short-run at fixed prices
- Managing risk
  - Enter into a forward agreement to guarantee the exchange rate
  - Use foreign currency options to lock in exchange rates if they move against you but benefit from rates if they move in your favor

22.25 Long-Run Exposure

- Long-run fluctuations come from unanticipated changes in relative economic conditions
- Could be due to changes in labor markets or governments
- More difficult to hedge
- Try to match long-run inflows and outflows in the currency
- Borrowing in the foreign country may mitigate some of the problems

22.26 Translation Exposure

- Income from foreign operations has to be translated back to U.S. dollars for accounting purposes, even if foreign currency is not actually converted back to dollars
- If gains and losses from this translation flowed through directly to the income statement, there would be significant volatility in EPS
- Current accounting regulations require that all cash flows be converted at the prevailing exchange rates with currency gains and losses accumulated in a special account within shareholders equity

22.27 Managing Exchange Rate Risk

- Large multinational firms may need to manage the exchange rate risk associated with several different currencies
- The firm needs to consider its net exposure to currency risk instead of just looking at each currency separately
- Hedging individual currencies could be expensive and may actually increase exposure

22.28 Political Risk

- Changes in value due to political actions in the foreign country
- Investment in countries that have unstable governments should require higher returns
- The extent of political risk depends on the nature of the business
  - The more dependent the business is on other operations within the firm, the less valuable it is to others
  - Natural resource development can be very valuable to others, especially if much of the ground work in developing the resource has already been done
- Local financing can often reduce political risk

Quick Quiz

- What does an exchange rate tell us?
- What is triangle arbitrage?
- What are absolute purchasing power parity and relative purchasing power parity?
- What are covered interest arbitrage and interest rate parity?
- What are uncovered interest parity and the International Fisher Effect?
- What are the two methods for international capital budgeting?
- What is the difference between short-run interest rate exposure and long-run interest rate exposure? How can you hedge each type?
- What is political risk and what types of business face the greatest risk?

23.1 Key Concepts and Skills

- Understand the types of volatility that companies can manage
- Understand how to develop risk profiles
- Understand the difference between forward contracts and futures contracts and how they are used for hedging
- Understand how swaps can be used for hedging
- Understand how options can be used for hedging

23.2 Chapter Outline

- Hedging and Price Volatility
- Managing Financial Risk
- Hedging with Forward Contracts
- Hedging with Futures Contracts
- Hedging with Swap Contracts
- Hedging with Option Contracts

23.3 Example: Disney's Risk Management Policy

- Disney provides stated policies and procedures concerning risk management strategies in its annual report
    - The company tries to manage exposure to interest rates, foreign currency, and the fair market value of certain investments
    - Interest rate swaps are used to manage interest rate exposure
    - Options and forwards are used to manage foreign exchange risk in both assets and anticipated revenues
    - Derivative securities are used only for hedging, not speculation

23.4 Hedging Volatility

- Recall that volatility in returns is a classic measure of risk
- Volatility in day-to-day business factors often leads to volatility in cash flows and returns
- If a firm can reduce that volatility, it can reduce its business risk
- Instruments have been developed to hedge the following types of volatility
    - Interest Rate
    - Exchange Rate
    - Commodity Price

23.5 Interest Rate Volatility

- Debt is a key component of a firm's capital structure
- Interest rates can fluctuate dramatically in short periods of time
- Companies that hedge against changes in interest rates can stabilize borrowing costs
- This can reduce the overall risk of the firm
- Available tools: forwards, futures, swaps, futures options and options

23.6 Exchange Rate Volatility

- Companies that do business internationally are exposed to exchange rate risk
- The more volatile the exchange rates, the more difficult it is to predict the firm's cash flows in its domestic currency
- If a firm can manage its exchange rate risk, it can reduce the volatility of its foreign earnings and do a better analysis of future projects
- Available tools: forwards, futures, swaps, futures options

23.7 Commodity Price Volatility

- Most firms face volatility in the costs of materials and in the price that will be received when products are sold
- Depending on the commodity, the company may be able to hedge price risk using a variety of tools
- This allows companies to make better production decisions and reduce the volatility in cash flows
- Available tools (depend on type of commodity): forwards, futures, swaps, futures options, options

23.8 The Risk Management Process

- Identify the types of price fluctuations that will impact the firm
- Some risks are obvious, others are not
- Some risks may offset each other, so it is important to look at the firm as a portfolio of risks and not just look at each risk separately
- You must also look at the cost of managing the risk relative to the benefit derived
- Risk profiles are a useful tool for determining the relative impact of different types of risk

23.9 Risk Profiles

- Basic tool for identifying and measuring exposure to risk
- Graph showing the relationship between changes in price versus changes in firm value
- Similar to graphing the results from a sensitivity analysis
- The steeper the slope of the risk profile, the greater the exposure and the more a firm needs to manage that risk

23.10 Reducing Risk Exposure

- The goal of hedging is to lessen the slope of the risk profile
- Hedging will not normally reduce risk completely
  - Only price risk can be hedged, not quantity risk
  - You may not want to reduce risk completely because you miss out on the potential upside as well
- Timing
  - Short-run exposure (transactions exposure) – can be managed in a variety of ways
  - Long-run exposure (economic exposure) – almost impossible to hedge, requires the firm to be flexible and adapt to permanent changes in the business climate

23.11 Forward Contracts

- A contract where two parties agree on the price of an asset today to be delivered and paid for at some future date
- Forward contracts are legally binding on both parties
- They can be tailored to meet the needs of both parties and can be quite large in size
- Positions
  - Long – agrees to buy the asset at the future date
  - Short – agrees to sell the asset at the future date
- Because they are negotiated contracts and there is no exchange of cash initially, they are usually limited to large, creditworthy corporations

23.12 Figure 23.7

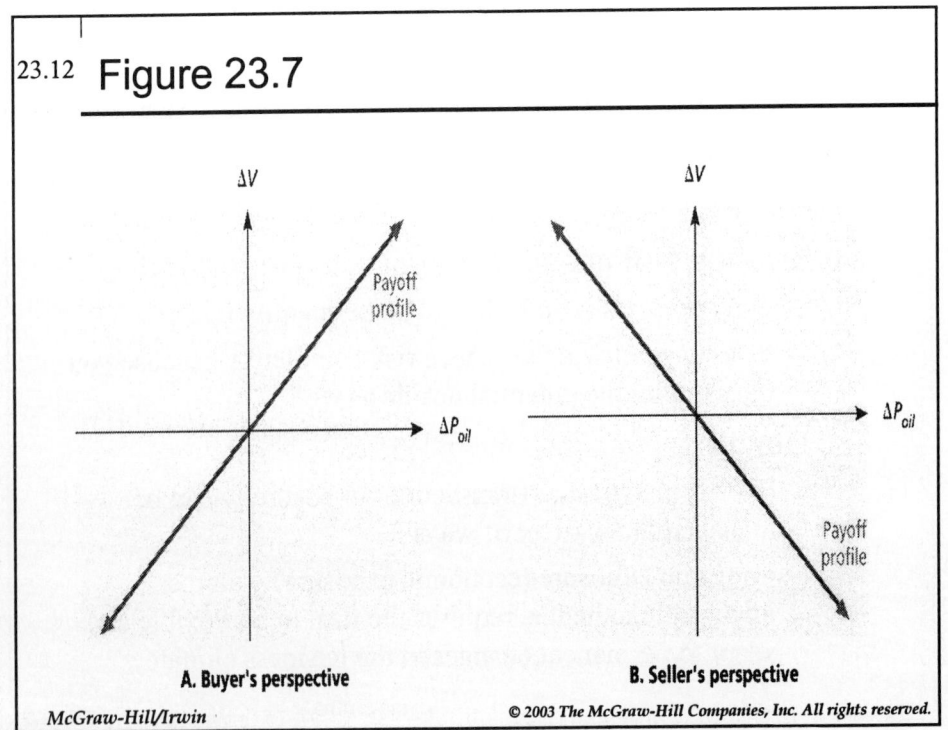

23.13 Hedging with Forwards

- Entering into a forward contract can virtually eliminate the price risk a firm faces
  - It does not completely eliminate risk unless there is no uncertainty concerning the quantity
- Because it eliminates the price risk, it prevents the firm from benefiting if prices move in the company's favor
- The firm also has to spend some time and/or money evaluating the credit risk of the counterparty
- Forward contracts are primarily used to hedge exchange rate risk

23.14 Futures Contracts

- Forward contracts traded on an organized securities exchange
- Require an upfront cash payment called margin
  - Small relative to the value of the contract
  - "Marked-to-market" on a daily basis
- Clearinghouse guarantees performance on all contracts
- The clearinghouse and margin requirements virtually eliminate credit risk

23.15 Futures Quotes

- See Table 23.1
- Commodity, exchange, size, quote units
  - The contract size is important when determining the daily gains and losses for marking-to-market
- Delivery month
  - Open price, daily high, daily low, settlement price, change from previous settlement price, contract lifetime high and low prices, open interest
  - The change in settlement price times the contract size determines the gain or loss for the day
    - Long – an increase in the settlement price leads to a gain
    - Short – an increase in the settlement price leads to a loss
  - Open interest is how many contracts are currently outstanding

23.16 Hedging with Futures

- The risk reduction capabilities of futures is similar to that of forwards
- The margin requirements and marking-to-market require an upfront cash outflow and liquidity to meet any margin calls that may occur
- Futures contracts are standardized, so the firm may not be able to hedge the exact quantity it desires
- Credit risk is virtually nonexistent
- Futures contracts are available on a wide range of physical assets, debt contracts, currencies and equities

23.17 Swaps

- A long-term agreement between two parties to exchange cash flows based on specified relationships
- Can be viewed as a series of forward contracts
- Generally limited to large creditworthy institutions or companies
- Interest rate swaps – the net cash flow is exchanged based on interest rates
- Currency swaps – two currencies are swapped based on specified exchange rates or foreign vs. domestic interest rates

23.18 Example: Interest Rate Swap

- Consider the following interest rate swap
  - Company A can borrow from a bank at 8% fixed or LIBOR + 1% floating (borrows fixed)
  - Company B can borrow from a bank at 9.5% fixed or LIBOR + .5% (borrows floating)
  - Company A prefers floating and Company B prefers fixed
  - By entering into the swap agreements, both A and B are better off then they would be borrowing from the bank and the swap dealer makes .5%

	Pay	Receive	Net
Company A	LIBOR + .5%	8.5%	-LIBOR
Swap Dealer w/A	8.5%	LIBOR + .5%	
Company B	9%	LIBOR + .5%	-9%
Swap Dealer w/B	LIBOR + .5%	9%	
Swap Dealer Net	LIBOR + 9%	LIBOR + 9.5%	+.5%

Figure 23.10

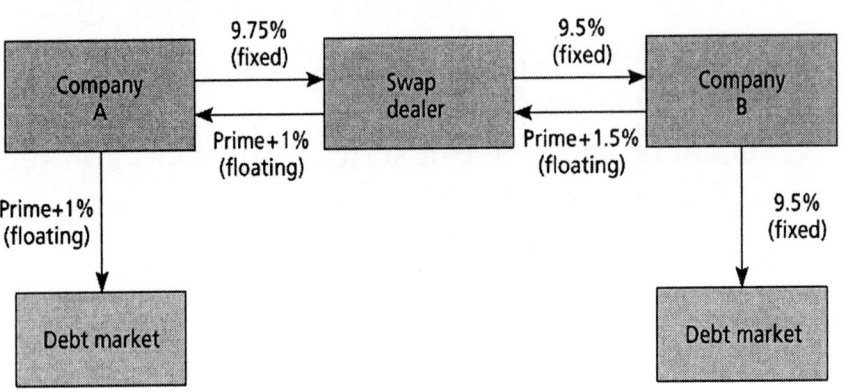

Company A borrows at prime plus 1% and swaps for a 9.75% fixed rate. Company B borrows at 9.5% fixed and swaps for a prime plus 1.5% floating rate.

Option Contracts

- The right, but not the obligation, to buy (sell) an asset for a set price on or before a specified date
  - Call – right to buy the asset
  - Put – right to sell the asset
  - Exercise or strike price – specified price
  - Expiration date – specified date
- Buyer has the right to exercise the option, the seller is obligated
  - Call – option writer is obligated to sell the asset if the option is exercised
  - Put – option writer is obligated to buy the asset if the option is exercised
- Unlike forwards and futures, options allow a firm to hedge downside risk, but still participate in upside potential
- Pay a premium for this benefit

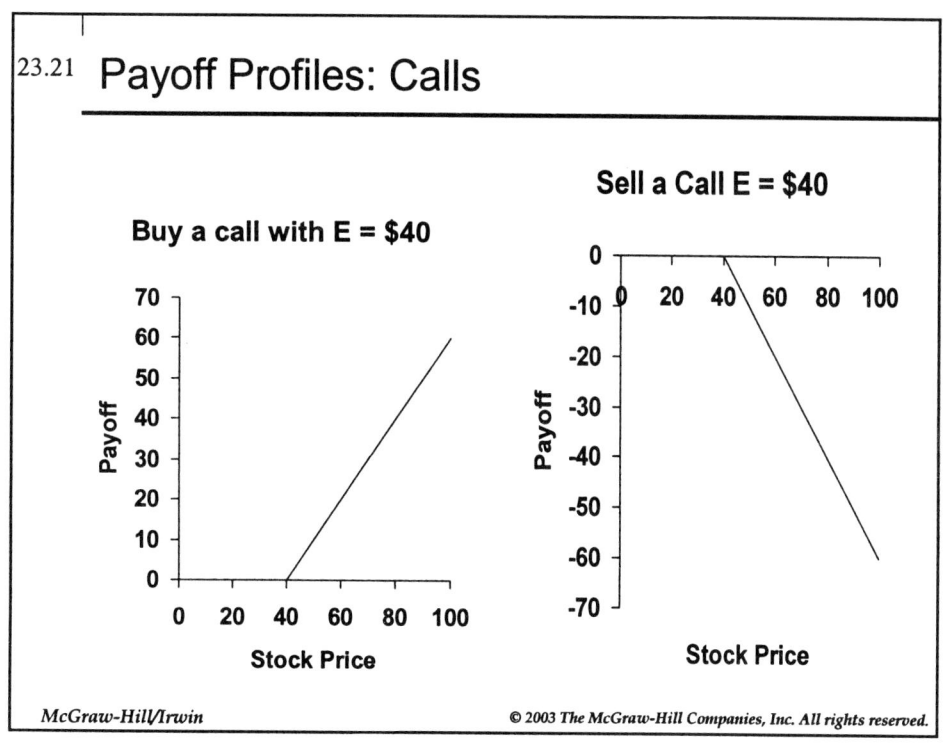
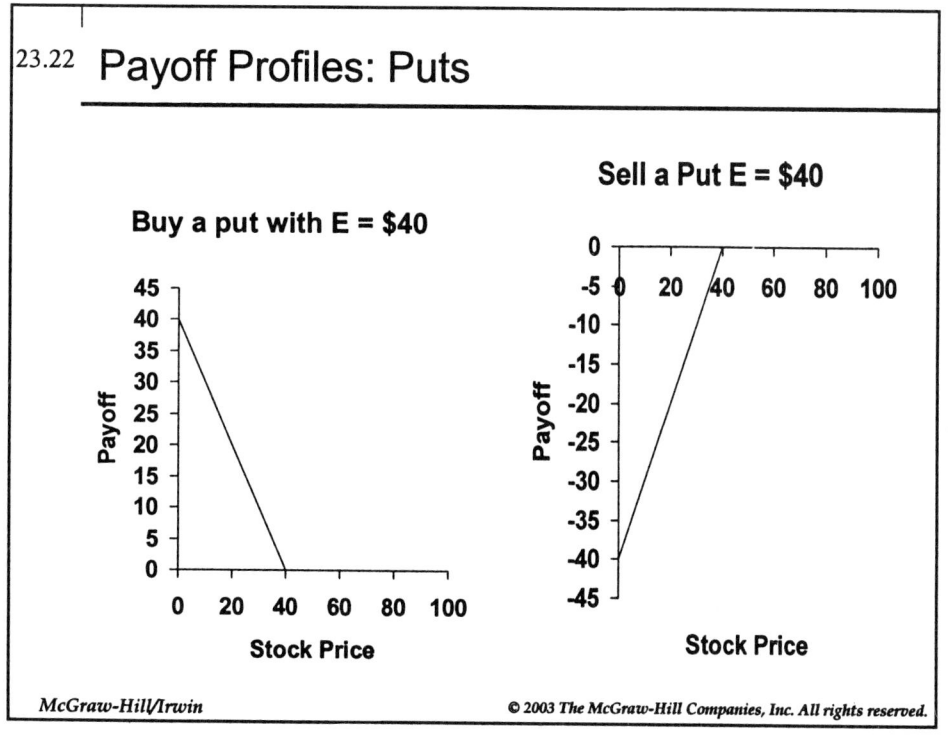

23.23 Hedging Commodity Price Risk with Options

- "Commodity" options are generally futures options
- Exercising a call
  - Owner of call receives a long position in the futures contract plus cash equal to the difference between the exercise price and the futures price
  - Seller of call receives a short position in the futures contract and pays cash equal to the difference between the exercise price and the futures price
- Exercising a put
  - Owner of put receives a short position in the futures contract plus cash equal to the difference between the futures price and the exercise price
  - Seller of put receives a long position in the futures contract and pays cash equal to the difference between the futures price and the exercise price

23.24 Hedging Exchange Rate Risk with Options

- May use either futures options on currency or straight currency options
- Used primarily by corporations that do business overseas
- US companies want to hedge against a strengthening dollar (receive fewer dollars when you convert foreign currency back to dollars)
- Buy puts (sell calls) on foreign currency
  - Protected if the value of the foreign currency falls relative to the dollar
  - Still benefit if the value of the foreign currency increases relative to the dollar
  - Buying puts is less risky

Hedging Interest Rate Risk with Options

- Can use futures options
- Large OTC market for interest rate options
- Caps, Floors, and Collars
  - Interest rate cap prevents a floating rate from going above a certain level (buy a call on interest rates)
  - Interest rate floor prevents a floating rate from going below a certain level (sell a put on interest rates)
  - Collar – buy a call and sell a put
    - The premium received from selling the put will help offset the cost of buying a call
    - If set up properly, the firm will not have either a cash inflow or outflow associated with this position

Quick Quiz

- What are the four major types of derivatives discussed in the chapter?
- How do forwards and futures differ? How are they similar?
- How do swaps and forwards differ? How are they similar?
- How do options and forwards differ? How are they similar?

24.1 Key Concepts and Skills

- Understand and be able to use Put-Call Parity
- Be able to use the Black-Scholes Option Pricing Model
- Understand the relationships between option premiums and stock price, time to expiration, standard deviation and the risk-free rate
- Understand how the OPM can be used to evaluate corporate decisions

24.2 Chapter Outline

- Put-Call Parity
- The Black-Scholes Option Pricing Model
- More on Black-Scholes
- Valuation of Equity and Debt in a Leveraged Firm
- Options and Corporate Decisions: Some Applications

24.3 Protective Put

- Buying the underlying asset and a put option to protect against a decline in the value of the underlying asset
- Pay the put premium to limit the downside risk
- Similar to paying an insurance premium to protect against potential loss
- Trade-off between the amount of protection and the price that you pay for the option

24.4 An Alternative Strategy

- You could buy a call option and invest the present value of the exercise price in a risk-free asset
- If the value of the asset increases, you can buy it using the call option and your investment
- If the value of the asset decreases, you let your option expire and you still have your investment in the risk-free asset

24.5 Comparing the Stratgies

	Value at Expiration	
Initial Position	$S < E$	$S \geq E$
Stock + Put	E	S
Call + PV(E)	E	S

- Stock + Put
  - If $S < E$, exercise put and receive E
  - If $S \geq E$, let put expire and have S
- Call + PV(E)
  - PV(E) will be worth E at expiration of the option
  - If $S < E$, let call expire and have investment, E
  - If $S \geq E$, exercise call using the investment and have S

24.6 Put-Call Parity

- If the two positions are worth the same at the end, they must cost the same at the beginning
- This leads to the put-call parity condition
  - $S + P = C + PV(E)$
- If this condition does not hold, there is an arbitrage opportunity
  - Buy the "low" side and sell the "high" side
- You can also use this condition to find any of the variables

24.7 Example: Finding the Call Price

- You have looked in the financial press and found the following information:
  - Current stock price = $50
  - Put price = $1.15
  - Exercise price = $45
  - Risk-free rate = 5%
  - Expiration in 1 year
- What is the call price?
  - $50 + 1.15 = C + 45 / (1.05)$
  - $C = 8.29$

24.8 Continuous Compounding

- Continuous compounding is generally used when working with option valuation
- Time value of money equations with continuous compounding
  - $EAR = e^{qt}$
  - $PV = FVe^{Rt}$
  - $FV = PVe^{-Rt}$
- Put-call parity with continuous compounding
  - $S + P = C + Ee^{-Rt}$

24.9 Example: Continuous Compounding

- What is the present value of $100 to be received in three months if the required return is 8%, with continuous compounding?
  - $PV = 100e^{-.08(3/12)} = 98.02$
- What is the future value of $500 to be received in nine months if the required return is 4%, with continuous compounding?
  - $FV = 500e^{.04(9/12)} = 515.23$

24.10 PCP Example: PCP with Continuous Compounding

- You have found the following information:
  - Stock price = $60
  - Exercise price = $65
  - Call price = $3
  - Put price = $7
  - Expiration is in 6 months
- What is the risk-free rate implied by these prices?
  - $S + P = C + Ee^{-Rt}$
  - $60 + 7 = 3 + 65e^{-R(6/12)}$
  - $.9846 = e^{-.5R}$
  - $R = -(1/.5)\ln(.9846) = .031$ or 3.1%

24.11 Black-Scholes Option Pricing Model

- The Black-Scholes model was originally developed to price call options
- $N(d_1)$ and $N(d_2)$ are found using the cumulative normal distribution tables

$$C = SN(d_1) - Ee^{-Rt}N(d_2)$$

$$d_1 = \frac{\ln\left(\frac{S}{E}\right) + \left(R + \frac{\sigma^2}{2}\right)t}{\sigma\sqrt{t}}$$

$$d_2 = d_1 - \sigma\sqrt{t}$$

24.12 Example: OPM

- You are looking at a call option with 6 months to expiration and an exercise price of $35. The current stock price is $45 and the risk-free rate is 4%. The standard deviation of underlying asset returns is 20%. What is the value of the call option?

$$d_1 = \frac{\ln\left(\frac{45}{35}\right) + \left(.04 + \frac{.2^2}{2}\right).5}{.2\sqrt{.5}} = 1.99$$

$$d_2 = 1.99 - .2\sqrt{.5} = 1.85$$

- Look up $N(d_1)$ and $N(d_2)$ in Table 24.3
- $N(d_1) = (.9761 + .9772)/2 = .9767$
- $N(d_2) = (.9671 + .9686)/2 = .9679$

$C = 45(.9767) - 35e^{-.04(.5)}(.9679)$

$C = \$10.75$

24.13 Example: OPM in a Spreadsheet

- Consider the previous example
- Click on the excel icon to see how this problem can be worked in a spreadsheet

24.14 Put Values

- The value of a put can be found by finding the value of the call and then using put-call parity
  - What is the value of the put in the previous example?
    - $P = C + Ee^{-Rt} - S$
    - $P = 10.75 + 35e^{-.04(.5)} - 45 = .06$
- Note that a put may be worth more if exercised than if sold, while a call is worth more "alive than dead" unless there is a large expected cash flow from the underlying asset

24.15 European vs. American Put Options

- The Black-Scholes model is strictly for European options
- It does not capture the early exercise value that sometimes occurs with a put
- If the stock price falls low enough, we would be better off exercising now rather than later
- A European option will not allow for early exercise and therefore, the price computed using the model will be too low relative to an American option that does allow for early exercise

24.16 Table 24.4

Input	Impact on Option Price from an Increase in Input		Common Name
	Call Options	Put Options	
Stock price (S)	+	−	Delta
Strike price (E)	−	+	
Time to expiration (t)	+	+	Theta
Standard deviation of return on stock (σ)	+	+	Vega
Risk-free rate (R)	+	−	Rho

Note: The effect of increasing the time to maturity is positive for an American put option, but the impact is ambiguous for a European put.

24.17 Work the Web Example

- There are several good options calculators on the Internet
- The Chicago Board Options Exchange has one such calculator
- Click on the web surfer to go to the calculator under trading tools and price the call option from the earlier example
  - S = $45; E = $35; R = 4%; t = .5; σ = .2

24.18 Varying Stock Price and Delta

- What happens to the value of a call (put) option if the stock price changes, all else equal?
- Take the first derivative of the OPM with respect to the stock price and you get delta.
  - For calls: Delta = $N(d_1)$
  - For puts: Delta = $N(d_1) - 1$
  - Delta is often used as the hedge ratio to determine how many options we need to hedge a portfolio

Figure 24.1

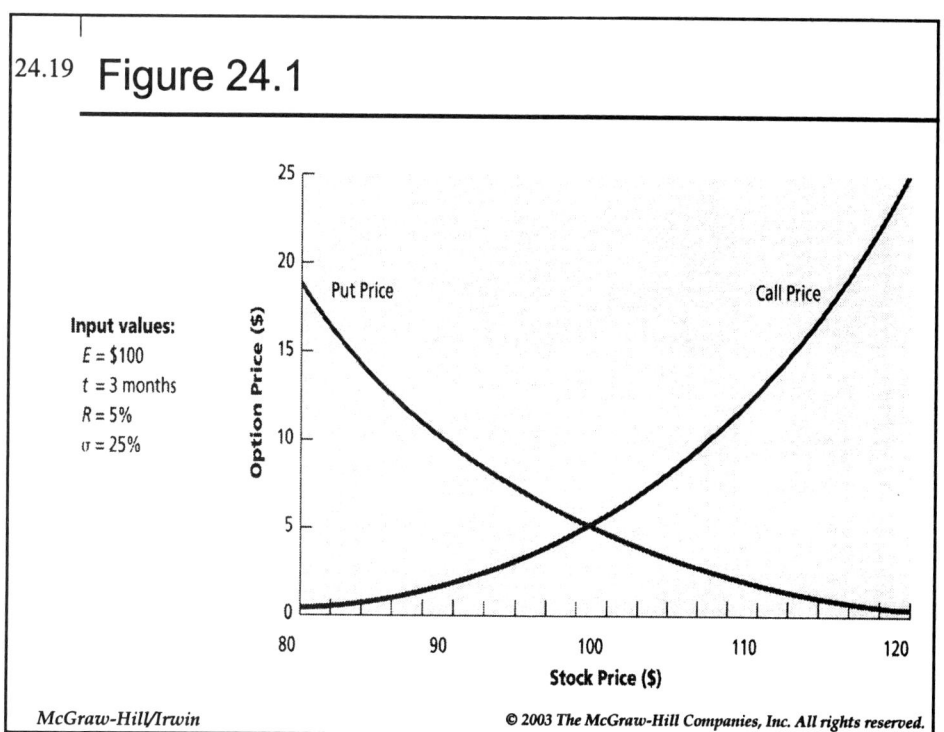

Input values:
E = $100
t = 3 months
R = 5%
σ = 25%

Example: Delta

- Consider the previous example:
  - What is the delta for the call option? What does it tell us?
    - $N(d_1) = .9767$
    - Change in option value is approximately equal to delta times change in stock price
  - What is the delta for the put option?
    - $N(d_1) - 1 = .9767 - 1 = -.0233$
  - Which option is more sensitive to changes in the stock price? Why?

24.21 Varying Time to Expiration and Theta

- What happens to the value of a call (put) as we change the time to expiration, all else equal?
- Take the first derivative of the OPM with respect to time and you get theta
- Options are often called "wasting" assets, because the value decreases as expiration approaches, even if all else remains the same
- Option value = intrinsic value + time premium

24.22 Figure 24.2

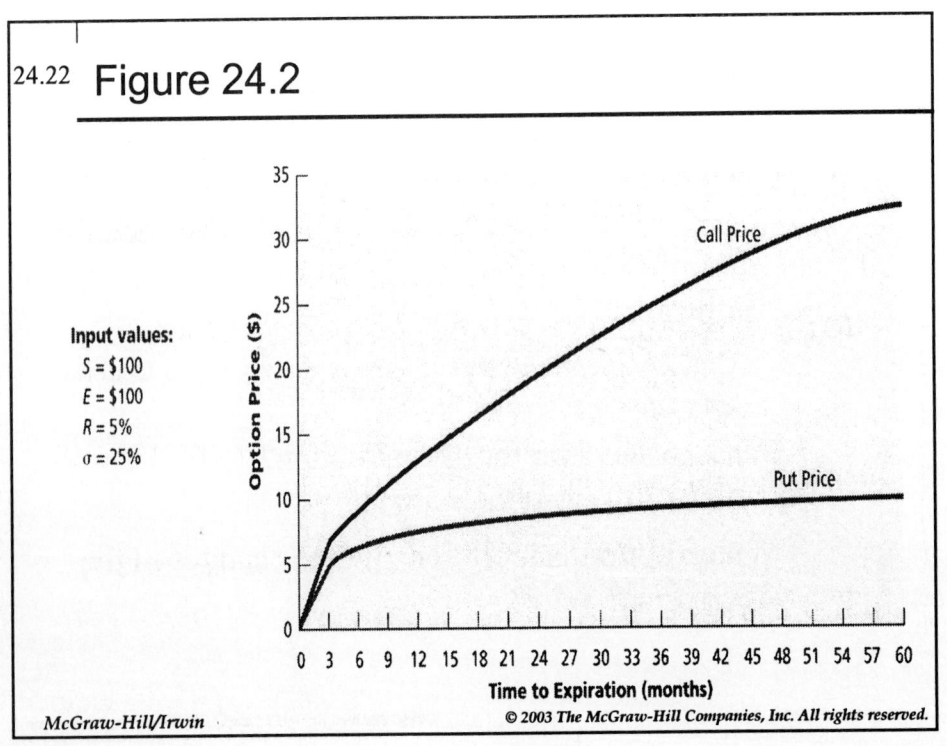

24.23 Example: Time Premiums

- What was the time premium for the call and the put in the previous example?
  - Call
    - C = 10.75; S = 45; E = 35
    - Intrinsic value = max(0, 45 − 35) = 10
    - Time premium = 10.75 − 10 = $0.75
  - Put
    - P = .06; S = 45; E = 35
    - Intrinsic value = max(0, 35 − 45) = 0
    - Time premium = .06 − 0 = $0.06

24.24 Varying Standard Deviation and Vega

- What happens to the value of a call (put) when you vary the standard deviation of returns, all else equal?
- Take the first derivative of the OPM with respect to sigma and you get vega
- Option values are <u>very</u> sensitive to changes in the standard deviation of return
- The greater the standard deviation, the more the call and the put are worth

24.25 Figure 24.3

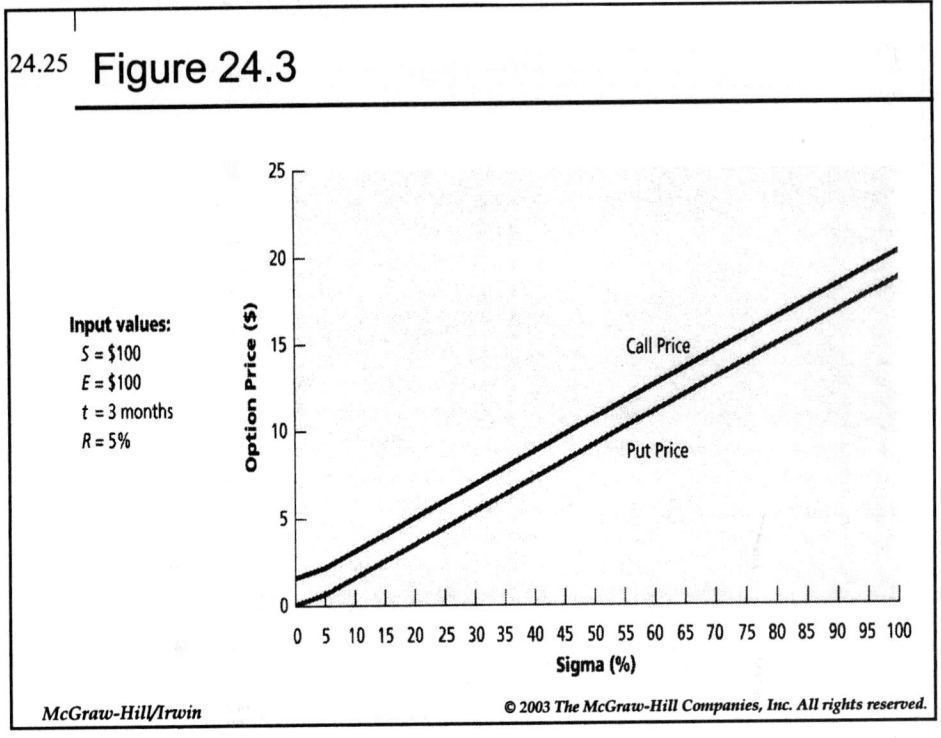

24.26 Varying the Risk-Free Rate and Rho

- What happens to the value of a call (put) as you vary the risk-free rate, all else equal?
- Take the first derivative of the OPM with respect to the risk-free rate and you get rho
- Changes in the risk-free rate have very little impact on options values over any normal range of interest rates

Figure 24.4

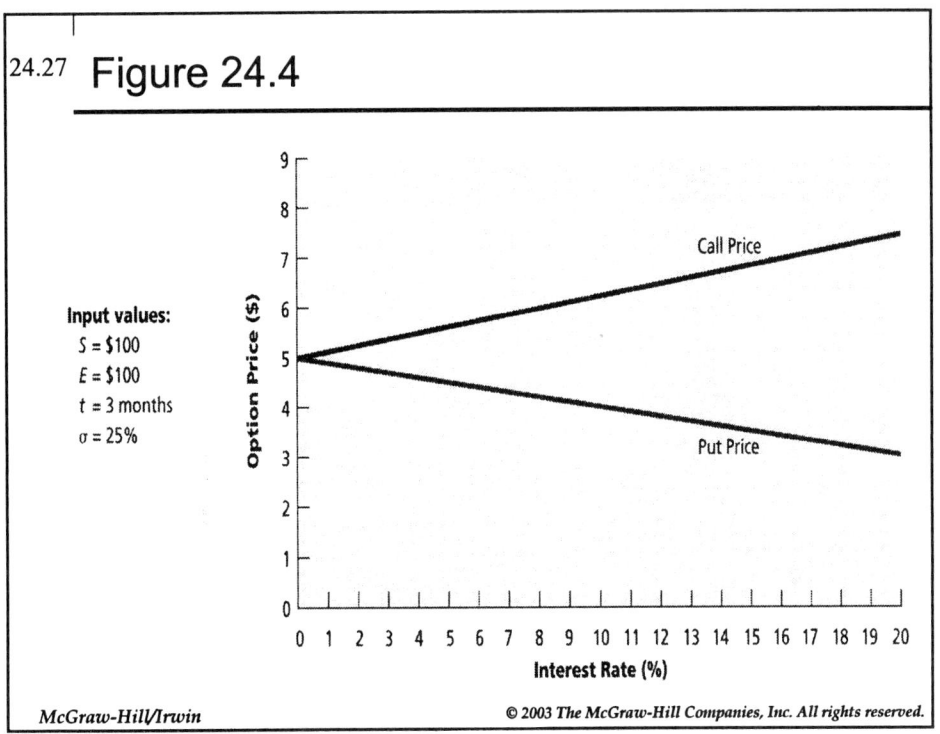

Input values:
S = $100
E = $100
t = 3 months
σ = 25%

Implied Standard Deviations

- All of the inputs into the OPM are directly observable, except for the expected standard deviation of returns
- The OPM can be used to compute the market's estimate of future volatility by solving for the standard deviation
- This is called the implied standard deviation
- Online options calculators are useful for this computation since there is not a closed form solution

24.29 Equity as a Call Option

- Equity can be viewed as a call option on the firm's assets whenever the firm carries debt
- The strike price is the cost of making the debt payments
- The underlying asset price is the market value of the firm's assets
- If the intrinsic value is positive, the firm can exercise the option by paying off the debt
- If the intrinsic value is negative, the firm can let the option expire and turn the firm over to the bondholder
- This concept is useful in valuing certain types of corporate decisions

24.30 Valuing Equity and Changes in Assets

- Consider a firm that has a zero coupon bond that matures in 4 years. The face value is $30 million and the risk-free rate is 6%. The current market value of the firm's assets is $40 million and the firm's equity is currently worth $18 million. Suppose the firm is considering a project with an NPV = $500,000.
  - What is the implied standard deviation of returns?
  - What is the delta?
  - What is the change in stockholder value?

24.31 PCP and the Balance Sheet Identity

- Risky debt can be viewed as a risk-free bond minus the cost of a put option
  - Value of risky bond = $Ee^{-Rt} - P$
- Consider the put-call parity equation and rearrange
  - $S = C + Ee^{-Rt} - P$
  - Value of assets = value of equity + value of a risky bond
- This is just the same as the traditional balance sheet identity
  - Assets = liabilities + equity

24.32 Mergers and Diversification

- Diversification is a frequently mentioned reason for mergers
- Is this a good reason from a stockholder perspective?
- Diversification reduces risk and therefore volatility
- Decreasing volatility decreases the value of an option
- Since equity can be viewed as a call option, should a merger increase or decrease the value of the equity *assuming diversification is the only benefit to the merger*?

24.33 Extended Example – Part I

- Consider the following two merger candidates
- The merger is for diversification purposes only with no synergies involved
- Risk-free rate is 4%

	Company A	Company B
Market value of assets	$40 million	$15 million
Face value of zero coupon debt	$18 million	$7 million
Debt maturity	4 years	4 years
Asset return standard deviation	40%	50%

24.34 Extended Example – Part II

- Use the OPM (or an options calculator) to compute the value of the equity
- Value of the debt = value of assets – value of equity

	Company A	Company B
Market Value of Equity	25.681	9.867
Market Value of Debt	14.319	5.133

Extended Example – Part III

- The asset return standard deviation for the combined firm is 30%
- Market value assets (combined) = 40 + 15 = 55
- Face value debt (combined) = 18 + 7 = 25

	Combined Firm
Market value of equity	34.120
Market value of debt	20.880

Total MV of equity of separate firms = 25.681 + 9.867 = 35.548

Wealth transfer from stockholders to bondholders = 35.548 – 34.120 = 1.428 (exact increase in MV of debt)

M&A Conclusions

- Mergers for diversification only transfer wealth from the stockholders to the bondholders
- The standard deviation of returns on the assets is reduced, thereby reducing the option value of the equity
- If management's goal is to maximize *stockholder* wealth, then mergers for reasons of diversification should not occur

24.37 Extended Example: Low NPV – Part I

- Stockholders may prefer low NPV projects to high NPV projects if the firm is highly leveraged and the low NPV project increases volatility
- Consider a company with the following characteristics
  - MV assets = 40 million
  - FV debt = 25 million
  - Debt maturity = 5 years
  - Asset return standard deviation = 40%
  - Risk-free rate = 4%

24.38 Extended Example: Low NPV – Part II

- Current market value of equity = $22.657 million
- Current market value of debt = $17.343 million

	Project I	Project II
NPV	$3	$1
MV of assets	$43	$41
Asset return standard deviation	30%	50%
MV of equity	$23.769	$25.339
MV of debt	$19.231	$15.661

Extended Example: Low NPV – Part III

- Which project should management take?
- Even though project B has a lower NPV, it is better for stockholders
- The firm has a relatively high amount of leverage
  - With project A, the bondholders share in the NPV because it reduces the risk of bankruptcy
  - With project B, the stockholders actually appropriate additional wealth from the bondholders for a larger gain in value

Extended Example: Negative NPV – Part I

- We've seen that stockholders might prefer a low NPV to a high one, but would they ever prefer a negative NPV?
- Under certain circumstances they might
- If the firm is highly leveraged, stockholders have nothing to lose if a project fails and everything to gain if it succeeds
- Consequently, they may prefer a very risky project with a negative NPV but high potential rewards

24.41 Extended Example: Negative NPV – Part II

- Consider the previous firm
- They have one additional project they are considering with the following characteristics
  - Project NPV = -$2 million
  - MV of assets = $38 million
  - Asset return standard deviation = 65%
- Estimate the value of the debt and equity
  - MV equity = $25.423 million
  - MV debt = $12.577 million

24.42 Extended Example: Negative NPV – Part III

- In this case, stockholders would actually prefer the negative NPV project over either of the positive NPV projects
- The stockholders benefit from the increased volatility associated with the project even if the expected NPV is negative
- This happens because of the large levels of leverage

24.43 Conclusions

- As a general rule, managers should not go around accepting low or negative NPV projects and passing up high NPV projects
- Under certain circumstances, however, this may benefit stockholders
  - The firm is highly leveraged
  - The low or negative NPV project causes a substantial increase in the standard deviation of asset returns

24.44 Quick Quiz

- What is put-call parity? What would happen if it doesn't hold?
- What is the Black-Scholes option pricing model?
- How can equity be viewed as a call option?
- Should a firm do a merger for diversification purposes only? Why or why not?
- Should management ever accept a negative NPV project? If yes, under what circumstances?

25.1 Key Concepts and Skills

- Be able to define the various terms associated with M&A activity
- Understand the various reasons for mergers and whether or not those reasons are in the best interest of shareholders
- Understand the various methods for a paying for an acquisition
- Understand the various defensive tactics that are available

25.2 Chapter Outline

- The Legal Forms of Acquisitions
- Taxes and Acquisitions
- Accounting for Acquisitions
- Gains from Acquisition
- Some Financial Side Effects of Acquisitions
- The Cost of an Acquisition
- Defensive Tactics
- Some Evidence on Acquisitions

25.3 Merger versus Consolidation

- Merger
  - One firm is acquired by another
  - Acquiring firm retains name and acquired firm ceases to exist
  - Advantage – legally simple
  - Disadvantage – must be approved by stockholders of both firms
- Consolidation
  - Entirely new firm is created from combination of existing firms

25.4 Acquisitions

- A firm can be acquired by purchasing voting shares of the firm's stock
- Tender offer – public offer to buy shares
- Stock acquisition
  - No stockholder vote required
  - Can deal directly with stockholders, even if management is unfriendly
  - May be delayed if some target shareholders hold out for more money – complete absorption requires a merger
- Classifications
  - Horizontal – both firms are in the same industry
  - Vertical – firms are different stages of the production process
  - Conglomerate – firms are unrelated

25.5 Takeovers

- Control of a firm transfers from one group to another
- Possible forms
    - Acquisition
        - Merger or consolidation
        - Acquisition of stock
        - Acquisition of assets
    - Proxy contest
    - Going private

25.6 Taxes

- Tax-free acquisition
    - Business purpose; not solely to avoid taxes
    - Continuity of equity interest – stockholders of target firm must be able to maintain an equity interest in the combined firm
    - Generally, stock for stock acquisition
- Taxable acquisition
    - Firm purchased with cash
    - Capital gains taxes – stockholders of target may require a higher price to cover the taxes
    - Assets are revalued – affects depreciation expense

25.7 Accounting for Acquisitions

- Pooling of interests accounting no longer allowed
- Purchase Accounting
  - Assets of acquired firm must be reported at fair market value
  - Goodwill is created – difference between purchase price and estimated fair market value of net assets
  - Goodwill no longer has to be amortized – assets are essentially marked-to-market annually and goodwill is adjusted and treated as an expense if the market value of the assets has decreased

25.8 Synergy

- The whole is worth more than the sum of the parts
- Some mergers create synergies because the firm can either cut costs or use the combined assets more effectively
- This is generally a good reason for a merger
- Examine whether the synergies create enough benefit to justify the cost

25.9 Revenue Enhancement

- Marketing gains
    - Advertising
    - Distribution network
    - Product mix
- Strategic benefits
- Market power

25.10 Cost Reductions

- Economies of scale
    - Ability to produce larger quantities while reducing the average per unit cost
    - Most common in industries that have high fixed costs
- Economies of vertical integration
    - Coordinate operations more effectively
    - Reduced search cost for suppliers or customers
- Complimentary resources

25.11 Taxes

- Take advantages of net operating losses
  - Carry-backs and carry-forwards
  - Merger may be prevented if the IRS believes the sole purpose is to avoid taxes
- Unused debt capacity
- Surplus funds
  - Pay dividends
  - Repurchase shares
  - Buy another firm
- Asset write-ups

25.12 Reducing Capital Needs

- A merger may reduce the required investment in working capital and fixed assets relative to the two firms operating separately
- Firms may be able to manage existing assets more effectively under one umbrella
- Some assets may be sold if they are redundant in the combined firm (this includes human capital as well)

25.13 General Rules

- Do not rely on book values alone – the market provides information about the true worth of assets
- Estimate only incremental cash flows
- Use an appropriate discount rate
- Consider transaction costs – these can add up quickly and become a substantial cash outflow

25.14 EPS Growth

- Mergers may create the appearance of growth in earnings per share
- If there are no synergies or other benefits to the merger, then the growth in EPS is just an artifact of a larger firm and is not true growth
- In this case, the P/E ratio should fall because the combined market value should not change
- There is no free lunch

25.15 Diversification

- Diversification, in and of itself, is not a good reason for a merger
- Stockholders can normally diversify their own portfolio cheaper than a firm can diversify by acquisition
- Stockholder wealth may actually decrease after the merger because the reduction in risk in effect transfers wealth from the stockholders to the bondholders

25.16 Cash Acquisition

- The NPV of a cash acquisition is
  - $NPV = V_B^* - \text{cash cost}$
- Value of the combined firm is
  - $V_{AB} = V_A + (V_B^* - \text{cash cost})$
- Often, the entire NPV goes to the target firm
- Remember that a zero-NPV investment is also desirable

25.17 Stock Acquisition

- Value of combined firm
  - $V_{AB} = V_A + V_B + \Delta V$
- Cost of acquisition
  - Depends on the number of shares given to the target stockholders
  - Depends on the price of the combined firm's stock after the merger
- Considerations when choosing between cash and stock
  - Sharing gains – target stockholders don't participate in stock price appreciation with a cash acquisition
  - Taxes – cash acquisitions are generally taxable
  - Control – cash acquisitions do not dilute control

25.18 Defensive Tactics

- Corporate charter
  - Establishes conditions that allow for a takeover
  - Supermajority voting requirement
- Targeted repurchase aka greenmail
- Standstill agreements
- Exclusionary self-tenders
- Poison pills (share rights plans)
- Leveraged buyouts

25.19 More (Colorful) Terms

- Golden parachute
- Poison put
- Crown jewel
- White knight
- Lockup
- Shark repellent
- Bear hug

25.20 Evidence on Acquisitions

- Shareholders of target companies tend to earn excess returns in a merger
  - Shareholders of target companies gain more in a tender offer than in a straight merger
  - Target firm managers have a tendency to oppose mergers, thus driving up the tender price
- Shareholders of bidding firms earn a small excess return in a tender offer, but none in a straight merger
  - Anticipated gains from mergers may not be achieved
  - Bidding firms are generally larger, so it takes a larger dollar gain to get the same percentage gain
  - Management may not be acting in stockholders best interest
  - Takeover market may be competitive
  - Announcement may not contain new information about the bidding firm

Quick Quiz

- What are the different methods for achieving a takeover?
- How do we account for acquisitions?
- What are some of the reasons cited for mergers? Which may be in stockholders' best interest and which generally are not?
- What are some of the defensive tactics that firms use to thwart takeovers?

26.1 Key Concepts and Skills

- Understand the basic lease terminology
- Understand the criteria for a capital lease vs. an operating lease
- Understand the typical incremental cash flows to leasing
- Be able to compute the net advantage to leasing
- Understand the good reasons for leasing and the dubious reasons for leasing

26.2 Chapter Outline

- Leases and Lease Types
- Accounting and Leasing
- Taxes, the IRS and Leases
- The Cash Flows from Leasing
- Lease or Buy?
- A Leasing Paradox
- Reasons for Leasing

26.3 Lease Terminology

- Lease – contractual agreement for use of an asset in return for a series of payments
- Lessee – user of an asset; makes payments
- Lessor – owner of the asset; receives payments
- Direct lease – lessor is the manufacturer
- Captive finance company – subsidiaries that lease products for the manufacturer

26.4 Types of Leases

- Operating lease
  - Shorter-term lease
  - Lessor is responsible for insurance, taxes and maintenance
  - Often cancelable
- Financial lease (capital lease)
  - Longer-term lease
  - Lessee is responsible for insurance, taxes and maintenance
  - Generally not cancelable
  - Specific capital leases
    - Tax-oriented
    - Leveraged
    - Sale and leaseback

Lease Accounting

- Leases are governed primarily by FASB 13
- Financial leases are essentially treated as debt financing
  - Present value of lease payments must be included on the balance sheet as a liability
  - Same amount shown on the asset as the "capitalized value of leased assets"
- Operating leases are still "off-balance-sheet" and do not have any impact on the balance sheet itself

Criteria for a Capital Lease

- If one of the following criteria is met, then the lease is considered a capital lease and must be shown on the balance sheet
  - Lease transfers ownership by the end of the lease term
  - Lessee can purchase asset at below market price
  - Lease term is for 75 percent or more of the life of the asset
  - Present value of lease payments is at least 90 percent of the fair market value at the start of the lease

26.7 Taxes

- Lessee can deduct lease payments for income tax purposes
  - Must be used for business purposes and not to avoid taxes
  - Term of lease is less than 80 percent of the economic life of the asset
  - Should not include an option to acquire the asset at the end of the lease at a below market price
  - Lease payments should not start high and then drop dramatically
  - Must survive a profits test
  - Renewal options must be reasonable and consider fair market value at the time of the renewal

26.8 Incremental Cash Flows

- After-tax lease payment (outflow)
  - Lease payment*(1 – T)
- Lost depreciation tax shield (outflow)
  - Depreciation * tax rate for each year
- Initial cost of machine (inflow)
  - Inflow because we save the cost of purchasing the asset now
- May have incremental maintenance, taxes or insurance depending on the type of lease and whether the leased asset is replacing one currently owned

26.9 Example: Lease Cash Flows

- ABC, Inc. needs some new equipment. The equipment would cost $100,000 if purchased and would be depreciated straight-line over 5 years. No salvage is expected. Alternatively, the company can lease the equipment for $25,000 per year. The marginal tax rate is 40%.
    - What are the incremental cash flows?
        - After-tax lease payment = 25,000(1 - .4) = 15,000 (outflow years 1 - 5)
        - Lost depreciation tax shield = (100,000/5)*.4 = 8,000 (outflow years 1 – 5)
        - Cost of machine = 100,000 (inflow year 0)

26.10 Lease or Buy?

- The company needs to determine whether it is better off borrowing the money and buying the asset or leasing
- Compute the NPV of the incremental cash flows
- Appropriate discount rate is the after-tax cost of debt since a lease is essentially the same risk as a company's debt

26.11 Net Advantage to Leasing

- The net advantage to leasing (NAL) is the same thing as the NPV of the incremental cash flows
  - If NAL > 0, the firm should lease
  - If NAL < 0, the firm should buy
- Consider the previous example. Assume the firm's cost of debt is 10%.
  - After-tax cost of debt = 10(1 - .4) = 6%
  - NAL = 3,116
- Should the firm buy or lease?

26.12 Work the Web Example

- Many people have to choose between buying and leasing a car
- Click on the web surfer to go to Kiplinger's
  - Go to more calculators and chose the lease vs. buy
  - Do the calculations for a $30,000 car, 5-year loan at 7% with monthly payments and a $3000 down payment. The available lease is for 3 years and requires a $550 per month payment with a $1000 security deposit and $1000 other upfront costs.

26.13 Good Reasons for Leasing

- Taxes may be reduced
- May reduce some uncertainty
- May have lower transaction costs
- May require fewer restrictive covenants
- May encumber fewer assets than secured borrowing

26.14 Dubious Reasons for Leasing

- Balance sheet, especially leverage ratios, may look better if the lease does not have to be accounted for on the balance sheet
- 100% financing – except leases normally do require either a down-payment or security deposit
- Low cost – some may try to compare the "implied" rate of interest to other market rates, but this is not directly comparable

26.15 Quick Quiz

- What is the difference between a lessee and a lessor?
- What is the difference between an operating lease and a capital lease?
- What are the requirements for a lease to be tax deductible?
- What are typical incremental cash flows and how do you determine the net advantage to leasing?
- What are some good reasons for leasing?
- What are some dubious reasons for leasing?